Walking in Divine Provision

BENCOM Publications
a division of World Missions Ministries

BOOKS BY DR. BENJAMIN AYIM ASARE

English Books

1. From Deliverance to Inheritance

2. Life is a Priceless Treasure

3. The Hand of the Diligent Will Rule

4. Discover your Ministry in the Local Church

5. The Anointing is in the Assignment

6. Thanksgiving, A Way of Lifestyle

7. The Unfolding Mysteries of the Voice of the Blood

8. The Pursuit of Power Versus Fruit

9. Dress for the Occasion

10. Walking in Divine Provision

Italian Books

7. La Vita è un Tesoro Inestimabiled

8. Dalla Liberazione all'Eredità

AVAILABLE FROM BENCOM PUBLICATIONS, AMAZON.COM AND OTHER RETAIL OUTLETS

Walking in

Divine
Provision

Dr. Benjamin Ayim Asare

BOOK TITLE:
Walking in Divine Provision

WRITTEN BY Dr. BENJAMIN AYIM ASARE
ISBN: 978-0-9575775-8-9
eBook ISBN: 978-1-7398468-1-7

First published in Italy in 2023 by **BENCOM**
Via Ghiberti, 1
28100 Novara
Italy

Email: bayimasare@yahoo.it
Email: focicatmissions@yahoo.com
www.benjaminayimasareministries.com

Acknowledgements:
Editing / Proofreading / Research: Dr. Jennifer Pateman
Layout & eBook Marketing: Dorothea Struhlik
Cover Design: Dr.P.
Cover Image Credit: www.PosterMyWall.com

❖

Table of Contents

❖

Foreword

*I*t is a great privilege for me to write about the book "WALKING IN DIVINE PROVISION." The Holy Spirit revealed some of the deepest revelations upon Apostle Benjamin Ayim Asare. How our Mighty Lord God fulfills our necessities when we have challenges and nothing in our hands, but faith.

Many times, we are hopeless and in mental stress, because we are human beings, our wisdom has limits; we think it is the end. But there is nothing more than our God who is miraculous. Remember you can be a source of blessing for others through prophetic words, as Elijah said to the widow: "For this is what the Lord, the God of Israel, says: 'The jar of flour will not be used up and the jug of oil will not run dry until the day the Lord sends rain on the land'" (1 King 17:14).

This book gives the new hope and strength to the readers who are depressed and facing the challenges of life. As you turn the pages, you will see the great power of Jehovah Jireh, that how He supplied to the prophets and believers who just looked at heaven.

Because our God is the Provider, He never lets His people down and puts his servant in the hands of the enemy, making them suffer in intolerable situations. When you are tempted, He will also provide the way out that you can endure it.

I encourage you to read this book and learn how to walk in Divine Provision.

Bishop Paul Dilshad Bhatti
President: Jesus Calls Church Ministries International
Sao Paulo Brazil
www.jccmint.org

❖

Introduction

Many different distractions and controversies have swept the church from depending on the God of heaven who is our source of life and provision. When the Lord asked Abraham to offer Isaac as a burnt offering on the hill of Moriah, he obeyed the command. Abraham believed that even if Isaac were sacrificed, God would provide for another son.

When Isaac asked his father, "Where is the lamb for the burnt offering?" Abraham said, "My son, God will provide a lamb for the burnt offering." The Lord–Will–Provide, *Jehovah Jireh,* carries the idea of God making provision, when He sees the need. So when the Lord saw the need of Abraham, He provided. And when He saw humanity's need for salvation, He provided His Son, Jesus Christ. God is the One who supplies our needs. He desires that His children's needs be met

Sometimes we forget about God's goodness and focus on all of our sufferings and complaints about lack instead, forgetting that our human strength cannot provide for our sufficiency. In fact we live in an era of tremendous financial instability, with rising debt, regular economic crises, and a worldwide increase in unemployment, famine, and homelessness.

Famine has broken out in many places of the globe. People are dying with hunger and malnutrition. A whole lot of economical instability grips many nations. Massive international debt and bankruptcy have paralyzed many nations. These difficult times have brought the fear of the unknown to many people, including Christians, to keep what they have (such as money, food, and clothing etc.), rather than giving it away to others who are in need.

These situations have birthed the spirit of self-fishiness and profiteering in people. Failing to share what they have, with those who do not have. For example, believers have forgotten that we have been told to ask our heavenly Father daily for our bread. Because asking Him for our daily bread motivates our faith, (day by day), knowing that every blessed day God will provide for us. Jesus taught us to pray for our daily bread. **"Give us this day our daily bread"** (Matthew 6:11 KJV).

In addition, God asked the children of Israel to pick the manna daily. They were asked not to pick more than what they could eat in a day. God hates hording and profiteering. We see through scripture that those who collected more manna than their daily quota (and kept it for the following day), their batch became rotten! Clearly God was not happy with those who decided to take enough for two days. We too are meant to trust God daily for our needs – "God give us this day our daily bread."

The fact that we are to ask God for our daily bread does not mean that we should not make any investments or savings for our future contingencies. Our God is the Lord, both of the present and the future. For us to walk in His divine provision, we must also plan for our lives. We have seen great famines throughout history that caused many economic challenges and death. Even now we are at the edge of a worldwide economic war.

To survive, we must depend upon the Holy Spirit to help us know what is ahead of us and so that we can fully prepare for the future. In the case of the children of Israel, God used Joseph in Egypt to store up foodstuffs for the nation of Egypt and the world at large. Through this divine wisdom the Hebrews were preserved from famine. We see the same in the book of Acts chapter 11, where the prophet Agabus prophesied that there was going to be a great famine throughout the entire world. This also helps the Church to be prepared in advance, in order to bring some relief.

The Church must understand the economical war that is ahead (of all humankind), according to the Word of God in the book of Revelation chapters 13 and 14, which teaches us that the beast has a mark that he tries to place on us. And we see that terrible wrath comes upon all those who take the mark. Christians have striven to understand the way this beast would place his mark on them, so that they would know what to refuse and be free of the wrath foretold.

The way to abundant life is to depend on and trust Jesus Christ, the living bread. He shall supply all your need according to His riches in glory. As you prayerfully read and meditate on this information, let your hope and faith rest upon the living Word, Jesus Christ, the Son of the living God.

❖

CHAPTER 1

Lord Give us this Day our Daily Bread

After this manner therefore pray ye: Our Father which art in heaven, Hallowed be thy name. Thy kingdom come, Thy will be done in earth, as it is in heaven. Give us this day our daily bread. And forgive us our debts, as we forgive our debtors. And lead us not into temptation, but deliver us from evil: For thine is the kingdom, and the power, and the glory, forever. Amen.

(Matthew 6:9-13 KJV)

Lack of daily bread has led many people into unpleasant situations and difficulties. Many people have become snared into trials and temptations due to a lack of daily bread. We have seen countless numbers of people who have become victims, humiliated, and even confined into prison because of the lack of daily bread. We have seen people arrested in various supermarkets and marketplaces for stealing food because of lack of daily bread.

Since the time of creation mankind has been moving from one place to another searching for their daily bread. Our cities, towns and villages are busy, occupied with the traffic of people and automobiles for the purpose of daily bread. The absence of daily bread brings frustration.

I Am the Bread of Life

Jesus makes the declaration "I am the Bread of Life" three times in John chapter six verses 35, 48 and 51. He is the real heavenly bread, the true life-sustaining power; anything else, regardless of its significance both past and present, is an inadequate substitute. To believe in Him means to partake of Him.

Partaking in the covenant blood of Jesus is the means of being joined to God and receiving the benefits and privileges of His life. Jesus Christ is the covenant sacrifice and God's provision for our sustenance. When we feed on Him through faith and obedience, we become partakers of the divine nature, which is life eternal. "By which have been given to us exceedingly great and precious promises, that through these you may be partakers of the divine nature, having escaped the corruption *that* is in the world through lust" (2 Peter 1:4).

Through the Holy Spirit's work, we receive His life and partake of His promises. "It is the Spirit who gives life; the flesh profits nothing. The words that I speak to you are spirit, and *they* are life" (John 6:63).

Jesus came to teach us how to receive our daily bread from our heavenly Father. Without God supplying our daily bread we cannot survive. In fact, Jesus Himself is the bread of life. He said, "I am the bread of life. Your fathers ate the manna in the wilderness and are dead. This is the bread, which comes down from heaven that one may eat of it and not die. I am the living bread, which came down from heaven. If anyone eats of this bread, he will live forever; and the bread that I shall give is My flesh, which I shall give for the life of the world" (John 6:48-51).

Bread from Heaven

This is the bread which came down from heaven – not as your fathers ate the manna, and are dead. He who eats this bread will live forever.

(John 6:58)

This is a month and a half after the children of Israel left Egypt. Although they were slaves while in Egypt, yet they had been well cared for. Now that they are in the wilderness, they forgot God's goodness and their suffering and began to complain about the lack of foodstuffs.

God tested the people to know their hearts by giving them a certain quota of the bread every day. "Then said the LORD unto Moses, Behold, I will rain bread from heaven for you; and the people shall go out and gather a certain rate every day, that I may prove them, whether they will walk in my law, or not. And it shall come to pass, that on the sixth day they shall prepare that which they bring in; and it shall be twice as much as they gather daily" (Exodus 16: 4-5 KJV).

God is the giver of all things. He supplied bread from heaven daily for the congregation of Israel. He supplied them bread according to the number of each family. The bread supply comes morning by morning in God's time, according to His plan.

The instruction of the supply was that it couldn't be stored up for future use, except for the Sabbath (Saturday), the day of rest. This was a miraculous demonstration of God's provision to meet the needs of His people. Each family has all that is needed.

Those who gathered did not lack nor had left over. "Then the children of Israel did so and gathered some more, some less. So, when they measured *it* by omers, he who gathered much had nothing left over, and he who gathered little had no lack. Every man had gathered according to each one's need" (Exodus 16:17-18). There was a restriction on the amount of heaven's bread that they should gather.

They can have an omer of the bread per a day – that is about 4 pints. The Lord's Prayer, "Give us day by day our daily bread" (Luke 11:3), is an illustration of the daily supply of the bread from heaven given to the congregation of Israel. The petition of bread day by day is act of faith in God. If we can trust God Day by day to supply our needs, we will not be preoccupied of the circumstances we may face in life. It means we will build confidence and hope in the Lord and depend absolutely in Him.

It is never God's intention for us to store food especially while others are starving to death. We have no right as God's children to keep food while friends and church members have nothing to eat. Jesus asked the disciples to keep food only when everyone was filled.

Any time God asks you to give out something, and then He wants to take what you have and gives you the best. "He takes away the first that He may establish the second" (Hebrews 10:9). God never allows you to lose anything unless He plans to return something better than what you had. "Jesus said, unless a grain of wheat falls into the ground and dies, it remains alone; but if it dies, it produces much grain" (John 12:24).

A Call to Eat Breakfast by the Sea

Jesus said to them, "Come and eat breakfast." Yet none of the disciples dared ask Him, "Who are You?" knowing that it was the Lord. Jesus then came and took the bread and gave it to them, and likewise the fish. This is now the third time Jesus showed Himself to His disciples after He was raised from the dead.

(John 21:12-14)

Jesus is our role model in terms of generosity, giving and provision. He is the one who supplies us with all things. We have been taught in the scriptures to be hospitable. After Jesus' death and resurrection, he paid a visit to Peter and the rest of the disciples who had returned to their secular occupations as fishermen.

The scripture says Jesus showed Himself to the disciples at the Sea of Tiberias. "But when the morning had now come,

17

Jesus stood on the shore; yet the disciples did not know that it was Jesus. Then Jesus said to them, 'Children, have you any food?' They answered Him, 'No.' And He said to them, 'Cast the net on the right side of the boat, and you will find *some*.' So, they cast, and now they were not able to draw it in because of the multitude of fish" (John 21:4-6).

Jesus came to the shore and prepared breakfast and called the disciples to come and eat. Jesus is generous all the time. He is a great provider.

> *Then, as soon as they had come to land, they saw a fire of coals there, and fish laid on it, and bread. Jesus said to them, "Bring some of the fish which you have just caught." Simon Peter went up and dragged the net to land, full of large fish, one hundred and fifty-three; and although there were so many, the net was not broken. Jesus said to them, "Come and eat breakfast." Yet none of the disciples dared ask Him, "Who are You?" – knowing that it was the Lord. Jesus then came and took the bread and gave it to them, and likewise the fish.*
>
> *(John 21:9-13)*

The miraculous catch of the fish and breakfast with their Lord and master convinced them of who He was, and yet left them too awed to spoil with words the wonder of His presence.

❖

CHAPTER 2

They Shall Eat
and have Some Left Over

*T*he Bible says famine broke out in Gilgal. Then Elisha, the prophet asked his servant to prepare food, one of them went into the field to gather herbs for the food but gathered harmful or poisonous leaves. As they were eating the food they cried out and called Elisha that there was death in the pot.

You may question, how they knew that there was death in the food. You must know that they were prophets, and it might be that God revealed it to them.

*And Elisha returned to **Gilgal**, and there was a famine in the land. Now the sons of the prophets were sitting before him; and he said to his servant, "Put on the large pot, and boil stew for the sons of the prophets." So one went* *out into the field to gather herbs, and found a wild vine, and gathered from it a lapful of wild gourds, and came and sliced them into the pot of stew, though they did not know what they were. Then they served it to the men to eat. Now it happened, as they were eating the stew, that they cried out and said, "Man of God, there is death in the pot!" And they could not eat it. So he said, "Then bring some **flour**." And he put it into the pot, and said, "Serve it to the people, that they may eat." And there was nothing harmful in the pot.*

(2 Kings 4:38-41)

Elisha then asked for flour and put it into the pot and there was nothing harmful in the pot. This is an amazing miracle that only God can perform. Now why Elisha should purify the stew with flour? Flour is the key element that bread is made from. Bread in the scriptures represents God's Word. It is the stuff of our spiritual life. Jesus is the bread of Life, and a type of the broken bread that we are reading in the scriptures. So, flour could represent the divinity of Christ and the representation of His nature or His Body.

For I received from the Lord that which I also delivered to you: that the Lord Jesus on the same night in which He was betrayed took bread; and when He had given thanks, He broke it and said, "Take, eat; this is My body which is broken for you; do this in remembrance of Me."

(1 Corinthians 11:23-24)

The Bread of the Firstfruits – More than Enough

*Then a man came from **Baal Shalisha**, and brought the man of God **bread of the firstfruits**, twenty loaves of*

barley bread, and newly ripened grain in his knapsack. And he said, "Give it to the people, that they may eat." But his servant said, "What? Shall I set this before one hundred men?" He said again, "Give it to the people, that they may eat; for thus says the LORD: 'They shall eat and have some left over.'" So he set it before them; and they ate and had some left over, according to the word of the LORD.
                                                    (2 Kings 4:42-44)

The above passage or story is a picture of Jesus coming to the world to supply our needs. A man from Baal Shalisha brought the man of God, Elisha bread of the firstfruits, twenty loaves of barley **bread**. The name Baal-shalisha consists of two parts. The first part is the familiar word *(ba'al)*, meaning lord or master: the verb 'baal' means to exercise dominion over; to own, control or be lord over. The ubiquitous noun *"ba'al"* means lord, master and even husband, and its feminine counterpart *"ba'ala"* means mistress or landlady.

Our dependency is totally and solely depending upon God, He is our resource. As I mentioned previously, in the time of Elisha, a great famine had depleted the land, and the servant of the prophets was instructed to prepare stew for the prophets. He then went to the field to gather herbs for the stew but unfortunately he also gathered wild gourds, which were harmful to course death.

Miraculously, the Man of God healed the pot of the stew with flour, which is symbolic of the deity of Christ Jesus. Christ is the bread of life and the supplier of the bread, so Jesus is our Baal Shalisha. As Elisha demonstrated the care for the daily provision of the people, so did Jesus, by multiplying the loaves and fish.

But Jesus said unto them, they need not depart; give ye them to eat. And they say unto him, we have here but five loaves, and two fishes. He said, Bring them hither to me. And he commanded the multitude to sit down on the grass, and took the five loaves, and the two fishes, and looking up to heaven, he blessed, and brake, and gave the loaves to his disciples, and the disciples to the multitude. And they did all eat, and were filled: and they took up of the fragments that remained twelve baskets full. And they that had eaten were about five thousand men, beside women and children.

(Matthew 14:16-21 KJV)

Jesus will Break the Limitations in your Life

In those days, the multitude being very great and having nothing to eat, Jesus called His disciples to Him and said to them, "I have compassion on the multitude, because they have now continued with Me three days and have nothing to eat. And if I send them away hungry to their own houses, they will faint on the way; for some of them have come from afar."

Then His disciples answered Him, "How can one satisfy these people with bread here in the wilderness?" He asked them, "How many loaves do you have?" And they said, "Seven." So He commanded the multitude to sit down on the ground. And He took the seven loaves and gave thanks, **broke** *them and gave them to His disciples to set before them; and they set them before the multitude. They also had a few small fish; and having blessed them, He said to set them also before them. So they ate and were filled,*

*and they took up seven large baskets of leftover fragments.
Now those who had eaten were about four thousand. And
He sent them away.*

(Mark 8:1-9)

Limitations can be setbacks, hindrances, failures, and disappointments in life. As a pastor I have come across many Christians who have gone through various kinds of limitations. I believe every believer must go through deliverance to break the grip of the enemy in their lives.

Jesus wanted to feed the multitude, but the bread and the fish were not enough to feed the congregation. He, therefore, thanked the Father and broke the limitation of the bread and the fish. For us to walk in God's abundance we must allow ourselves to go through the process of brokenness.

Obedience is one of the keys to walk in God's total abundance. For example, God wanted to save a widow and the son from famine. He sent His prophet, Elijah to the widow who was nearly without foodstuffs and asked her last food to be served to Elijah. If she did, God would give her an unfailing provision. The woman overcame her fear, responded in faith, and God was faithful to His promise. Do not fear when the Lord asks you to give. Give to God first in all things and you will never be disappointed.

Yes, back at Bible College a visiting pastor came from Singapore to minister to us, the hosting pastor asked the students to sow seed to the visiting pastor. That very day I was having only fifty dollars ($50), which I needed to buy two books for my thesis report and the balance for foodstuffs.

It was like an on-going war in my mind, should I give or not? If I give, how could I buy the books, what would I eat within the week? Finally, I obeyed the Lord and gave the ($50), after the class, I was going to my residence then I had a phone call from one of my elders in Italy he said, "I have sent you two hundred and fifty dollars, take this number for withdrawal." How much did you say? I exclaimed! "Two hundred and fifty dollars" I said thank you very much.

Then I began to praise and thank God for His faithfulness. When you give to the Lord you will never be disadvantage. "Honour the LORD with your possessions, and with the first fruits of all your increase; so, your barns will be filled with plenty, and your vats will overflow with new wine" (Proverbs 3:9-10).

Then the word of the LORD came to him, saying, "Arise, go to Zarephath, which belongs to Sidon, and dwell there. See, I have commanded a widow there to provide for you." So he arose and went to Zarephath. And when he came to the gate of the city, indeed a widow was there gathering sticks. And he called to her and said, "Please bring me a little water in a cup, that I may drink." And as she was going to get it, he called to her and said, "Please bring me a morsel of bread in your hand." So she said, "As the LORD your God lives, I do not have bread, only a handful of flour in a bin, and a little oil in a jar; and see, I am gathering a couple of sticks that I may go in and prepare it for myself and my son, that we may eat it, and die."

And Elijah said to her, "Do not fear; go and do as you have said, but make me a small cake from it first, and bring it to

*me; and afterward make some for yourself and your son.
For thus says the LORD God of Israel: 'The bin of flour
shall not be used up, nor shall the jar of oil run dry, until
the day the LORD sends rain on the earth.'" So she went
away and did according to the word of Elijah; and she and
he and her household ate for many days. The bin of flour
was not used up, nor did the jar of oil run dry, according
to the word of the LORD which He spoke by Elijah.*

(1 Kings 17:8-16)

Anytime God asks you to give, it is to your advantage
– not God's. When you give to God, you are opening doors
for Him to bless you. Remember, it was not about Elijah that
God wanted to feed but the Zarephath widow and the son.
God had fed His servant the prophet, Elijah by the ravens so
He could have fed him again by any other means. God wants
you to give your money, time, talent, and gifts in order to
bless you.

*Then the word of the LORD came to him, saying, "Get
away from here and turn eastward, and hide by the Brook
Cherith, which flows into the Jordan. And it will be that
you shall drink from the brook, and I have commanded the
ravens to feed you there." So he went and did according to
the word of the LORD, for he went and stayed by the Brook
Cherith, which flows into the Jordan. The ravens brought
him bread and meat in the morning, and bread and meat
in the evening; and he drank from the brook.*

(1 Kings 17:2-6)

The second miracle of Elijah was to restore to life the
dead son of the widow of Zarephath. God always wants

to give to His children. "Beloved, I wish above all things that thou mayest prosper and be in health, even as thy soul prospereth" (3 John 1:2 KJV). God is a God of abundance, and He wants to see you blessed. His desire is for your house to be in order, debt-free, stress free, providing for your family, accomplishing all your God-given objectives, and giving generously, so the Kingdom of God can be established in your community and throughout the world.

Every Life Begins with Seed Principles

Understanding the principles of harvest or financial increase is a great tool to overcome famine. Everything God has given to humankind is based on seed principles. If you want to experience the blessing of seedtime and harvest then, it is time to change your thinking to that of a sower's mentality.

> *Then He spoke many things to them in parables, saying: "Behold, a sower went out to sow. And as he sowed, some seed fell by the wayside; and the birds came and devoured them. Some fell on stony places, where they did not have much earth; and they immediately sprang up because they had no depth of earth. But when the sun was up, they were scorched, and because they had no root they withered away. And some fell among thorns, and the thorns sprang up and choked them. But others fell on good ground and yielded a crop: some a hundredfold, some sixty, some thirty. He who has ears to hear, let him hear!"*
>
> *(Matthew 13:3-9)*

A crop can be harvested by anybody, it may even be destroyed by either drought or storms, but you cannot destroy the power of its seed. If the seed is still in the ground, you have another thing coming. We need to learn to sow our seeds. Whenever we eat our seed, we miss out on the cream of the crop and all that, which would have come forth from that seed if it had been planted and allowed to germinate and produce fruit.

This is because in every seed, potentially speaking, there is uncountable fruit and immeasurable juice that can be a blessing to many people, and yet at the same time, one still has more seeds to sow. Do not eat your seed. Anytime you find a good land or soil do not hesitate to sow. For example, the children of Israel planted their seeds in lands, which were not theirs – Egypt, but they received the greatest part of the harvest when they were leaving. "The LORD had made the Egyptians friendly toward the people of Israel, and they gave them whatever they asked for. In this way they carried away the wealth of the Egyptians when they left Egypt" (Exodus 12:36 CEV).

Do not Give God the Surplus

Do not wait until you have more before you give. That is not how God's Kingdom principles work. Do not say when everything goes on well. When I have a good job – good pay. If you are always waiting for a convenient time, you will never sow. "He who observes the wind will not sow, and he who regards the clouds will not reap. As you do not know what the way of the wind is, *Or* how the bones *grow* in the womb of her who is with child, so you do not know the works of God who makes everything. In the morning sow your seed, for you do not know which will prosper, either

27

this or that, or whether both alike will be good" (Ecclesiastes 11:4-6).

Fear can hinder your giving. In 1 Kings 17, God wanted to bless the widow not Elijah. But the widow was afraid, because of the foodstuff. Now do not judge this widow too quickly. How many times has God spoken to you about sowing seed and you have been not obedient? The woman operated in fear – the fear of not having enough. Many people look what is in their hands as harvest, but God sees it as a seed. What is in God's hand always is a harvest. When God gives to you it becomes a seed again – then it continues.

Therefore, do not withhold the seed God has given you, sow it and at the appropriate time (if you do not loose heart), you shall reap and walk in God's abundance.

❖

CHAPTER 3

Why Leaving
the House of Bread?

Now it came to pass, in the days when the judges ruled, that there was a famine in the land. And a certain man of Bethlehem, Judah, went to dwell in the country of Moab, he and his wife and his two sons. The name of the man was Elimelech, the name of his wife was Naomi, and the names of his two sons were Mahlon and Chilion – Ephrathites of Bethlehem, Judah. And they went to the country of Moab and remained there. Then Elimelech, Naomi's husband, died; and she was left, and her two sons. Now they took wives of the women of Moab: the name of the one was Orpah, and the name of the other Ruth. And they dwelt there about ten years. Then both Mahlon and Chilion also died; so the woman survived her two sons and her husband.

(Ruth 1:1-5)

Throughout history, famine, recession, and war has displaced many nations, ethnic groups and people from one place of origin to another. On this notion, human migration has caused a great detriment to the world that we live in today. Decision-making is a profound thing in life. The moment you decide to travel or carry out an assignment, it shapes your life and destiny, either for good or for bad. Decision-making is personal; it is yours alone and not in any other person's hands.

Choices are inalienable rights given to us by our heavenly Father. We have a choice to make in our walk with God. Sometimes Christians do not have the Word of God and the Spirit's guidance, or they overlook and ignore the voice of God in their crucial moments, then make poor choices.

In the above passage of scripture, the family of Elimelech paid a heavy price for their decision. Naomi was conscious of the inevitable frustrations and disappointments, which are definite roadblocks to achievements. The Word of God makes Christians aware of how our faithfulness enables God to turn tragedy into victory. We see through the pages of the Scriptures how humankind's adversity becomes God's opportunity to advance His great redemptive and Kingdom purpose.

"Now it came to pass, in the days when the judges ruled, that there was a famine in the land. And a certain man of Bethlehem, Judah, went to dwell in the country of Moab, he and his wife and his two sons." Bethlehem means *house of bread*. Elimelech and the family went to dwell in the country of Moab to seek temporary relief. The Moabites were enemies of God and of Israel. God had foreworn the children of Israel not to allow them to enter their congregation because they hired Balaam to curse Israel when they were on their way to the Promised Land.

An Ammonite or Moabite shall not enter the assembly of the LORD; even to the tenth generation none of his descendants shall enter the assembly of the LORD forever, because they did not meet you with bread and water on the road when you came out of Egypt, and because they hired against you Balaam the son of Beor from Pethor of Mesopotamia, to curse you. Nevertheless, the LORD your God would not listen to Balaam, but the LORD your God turned the curse into a blessing for you, because the LORD your God loves you. You shall not seek their peace nor their prosperity all your days forever.

(Deuteronomy 23:3-6)

Furthermore, the Ammonites and Moabites were the descendants of Lot as the result of an act of incest.

Then Lot went up out of Zoar and dwelt in the mountains, and his two daughters were with him; for he was afraid to dwell in Zoar. And he and his two daughters dwelt in a cave. Now the firstborn said to the younger, "Our father is old, and there is no man on the earth to come in to us as is the custom of all the earth. Come, let us make our father drink wine, and we will lie with him, that we may preserve the lineage of our father." So they made their father drink wine that night. And the firstborn went in and lay with her father, and he did not know when she lay down or when she arose. It happened on the next day that the firstborn said to the younger, "Indeed I lay with my father last night; let us make him drink wine tonight also, and you go in and lie with him, that we may preserve the lineage of our father."

Then they made their father drink wine that night also. And the younger arose and lay with him, and he did not know when she lay down or when she arose. Thus both the daughters of Lot were with child by their father. The firstborn bore a son and called his name Moab; he is the father of the Moabites to this day. And the younger, she also bore a son and called his name Ben-Ammi; he is the father of the people of Ammon to this day.

(Genesis 19:30-38)

The Consequences of Leaving a Place God Has Appointed

The recession that came to Italy 2007 had displaced many citizens and immigrants who were in Italy to various places in Europe and beyond. The most compelling facts were the immigrants who did not lose their jobs but abandoned their work because they wanted to change environment and have regretted it. Others left because they wanted their children to learn English. These children were born and bred in Italy, but they thought that speaking in just one language would not make a person successful.

Following the crowd has become one pertinent issue in the life of Africans. Many people cannot decide for their own lives. This recession has caused breakdown in families and tremendous effects on the churches in Italy. Many denominations have closed their churches because they could not afford to meet their expenditures.

Most of the churches that were under mortgages had lost their buildings or property due to lack of finance. Majorities of these Christians who followed the crowd have also regretted and are now living between two opinions. The high cost and standard of living is threatening them in the UK and in other parts of Europe compared to Italy. Are they returning to Italy or staying to face the detriment of the conditions of their new discoveries?

Decision and Determination

Decision-making is a human prerogative; we alone have the potential of choice and to make decisions. Being able to plan is an enormous privilege. However, many people have great difficulty making decisions; some cannot make decisions at all and continue to be wallflowers in life. Decisions we make put us in charge of our lives. Every time we decide, we find out who we really are. Our own priorities and values are reinforced and connect us to what we believe is the rightful course of action. Successful lives are directly proportionate to a willingness to make rightful decisions. Full participation and commitment to a choice is always required.

These immigrants who have lived in Italy over two or three decades have put the physical ahead of the spiritual and went on to experience devastation. Truly many left because they lost their jobs and that is okay, they had no option but to seek for new opportunities to make a living. Leaving God's appointed position; we set out a course toward spiritual and physical ruin. When we go to Moab – the world or stray away from God's place of appointment, it is the initiation of sinking spiritually.

We became less effective as witnesses of Christ, lose the joy of God, and eventually are polluted by the worldly system. In fact, many of our church members who were on fire for the Lord and left have confessed that they can no longer even pray. Many are not attending church anymore due to long hours they make at their work place. Many must work throughout the week without a resting day. Their Christian life has begun to fall apart.

> *For what shall it profit a man, if he shall gain the whole world, and lose his own soul?*
>
> *(Mark 8:36 KJV)*

We blame circumstances, but we are the ones to be blamed. When you run away from a problem, you take your sinful heart with you. You may be in a new location and have a new situation, but the problem will resurface. A change in geography can never change attitudes unless a change of heart and character occurs.

Do your Best in any Circumstances

Remember, as a child of God, the circumstances we face in life are mostly caused by the enemy. Satan, our archenemy, he delights in diminishing God's purposes for our lives. Forces of darkness lurk in the shadows, whispering their lies, lying in wait for opportunities to rob mankind. For example, in the story of Joseph, Jacob's son, he went through unpleasant circumstances in life. Yet God was with him to turn the afflictions into victories. In times of hardship, we are to endure and allow God to finish His course.

Joseph finally became governor and second in command in Egypt. "And Pharaoh said to his servants, 'Can we find such a one as this, a man in whom is the Spirit of God?' Then Pharaoh said to Joseph, 'Inasmuch as God has shown you all this, there is no one as discerning and wise as you. You shall be over my house, and all my people shall be ruled according to your word; only regarding the throne will I be greater than you.' And Pharaoh said to Joseph, 'See, I have set you over all the land of Egypt'" (Genesis 41:38-41). Joseph's obedience fulfilled the promised God gave to Abraham.

> *Then He said to Abram: "Know certainly that your descendants will be strangers in a land that is not theirs, and will serve them, and they will afflict them four hundred years. And also the nation whom they serve I will judge; afterward they shall come out with great possessions."*
> *(Genesis 15:13-14)*

Through the interpretation of Pharaoh's dream by Joseph, God preserved the land and provided for the Egyptians, and for the entire family of Jacob. When he heard that there was grain in Egypt, he sent his children to go down to Egypt to buy foodstuffs. Through that Jacob and his family moved from the land of Canaan to Egypt to fulfill the promise of God. Through the famine, God's purpose was fulfilled. God always provides for His children whenever there is scarcity. God assures us that He is the great provider, and then we are to depend upon Him in all circumstances in life.

Joseph's brothers sold him, but God was in it. Satan is not all knowing he can set up evil schemes to cause pains in our lives but if we stand firm in the Lord, victory is ours in the long run. Joseph said this to his brothers:

And Joseph said to his brothers, "Please come near to me." So they came near. Then he said: "I am Joseph your brother, whom you sold into Egypt. But now, do not therefore be grieved or angry with yourselves because you sold me here; for God sent me before you to preserve life. For these two years the famine has been in the land, and there are still five years in which there will be neither plowing nor harvesting. And God sent me before you to preserve a posterity for you in the earth, and to save your lives by a great deliverance. So now it was not you who sent me here, but God; and He has made me a father to Pharaoh, and lord of all his house, and a ruler throughout all the land of Egypt."

(Genesis 45:4-8)

The Necessity of Saving and Investment

To walk in God's divine provision, we must also plan for our future. A believer must learn to be a wise steward. We must be good managers in all that God has entrusted in our hands. For example, if you are a worker; you must at least be able to save 20% of your income. The savings or the investment you make would help you for the future contingencies. Making savings would add value to your capital and assist you in future.

We have all seen the result of the epidemic of the COVID-19, apart from the death of many souls; a lot of people struggled to live, because of a lack of food or finance. People who had enough foodstuffs and money were without pressure. Through the help of the Holy Spirit, we can discern the future and plan for our lives.

To survive, we must depend upon the Holt Spirit to help us know what is ahead of us so that we can fully prepare for the future. In the case of the children of Israel, God used Joseph in Egypt to store up food staffs for the nation of Egypt and the world at large. Through this divine wisdom the Hebrews were preserved from the famine.

We see the same in the book of Acts chapter 11 that the prophet Agabus prophesied that there was going to be a great famine throughout the world. This helps the church to be prepared ahead of time, to bring relief to the church. "During this time some prophets came down from Jerusalem to Antioch. One of them, named Agabus, stood up and through the Spirit predicted that a severe famine would spread over the entire Roman world. (This happened during the reign of Claudius.) The disciples, as each one was able, decided to supply help for the brothers and sisters living in Judea. This they did, sending their gift to the elders by Barnabas and Saul" (Acts 11:27-30 NIV).

We are living in the age of economical war. To understand this economic war, we must go to the Bible. It is important that we understand the ascension of the power bases and their present influence. Understanding that economics is the primary driving force of world affairs at the end of the age helps us to understand how the beast looks to gain dominance through commerce by controlling the "buying, selling and trading."

The book of Revelation chapter 13 teachers us that the beast has a mark which he tries to place upon us. "He causes all, both small and great, rich and poor, free and slave, to receive a mark on their right hand or on their foreheads, and that no one may buy or sell except one who has the mark or the name of the beast, or the number of his name" (Revelation 13:16-17).

We see that terrible wrath comes upon all who take the mark. Believers have striven to understand the way this beast would place his mark on them so that they would know what to refuse and be free of the wrath foretold. However, understanding how he places the mark is not as important as understanding the spiritual power behind the mark. "And the third angel followed them, saying with a loud voice, If any man worship the beast and his image, and receive his mark in his forehead, or in his hand, The same shall drink of the wine of the wrath of God, which is poured out without mixture into the cup of his indignation; and he shall be tormented with fire and brimstone in the presence of the holy angels, and in the presence of the Lamb" (Revelation 14:9-10 KJV).

Our major victory over the antichrist and the mark of the beast is the protection power of the Holy Spirit. Again, the believers must seek for the gift of wisdom to discern what is ahead of us and make proper plans towards the future. Savings and investment must be an integral part of the Christian life. Because to walk in God's divine provision we must also acquire proper planning and wisdom.

❖

CHAPTER 4

Discover How-to Walk-in God's Abundance

*B*ut seek first the kingdom of God and His righteousness, and all these things shall be added to you.

(Matthew 6:33)

There are principles or keys you need to engage to walk in God's abundance. You must admit that any abundance outside of God is limited or temporary. The Lord is the source of divine abundance, and your goal should be to stay connected with Him.

To walk in His abundance, you must desire and seek the Kingdom of God first. That means, things that are so dear to you must be a secondary matter. The Kingdom of God must be your priority and life pursuit. Here the term *righteousness* has the sense of seeking all of God's spiritual blessings, favour, image, and rewards. We see in this verse not only a broad New Testament application of the term but also, more importantly, its priority to life.

This dovetails perfectly with the hunger-and-thirst metaphor in the Beatitudes, "Blessed *are* those who hunger and thirst for righteousness, for they shall be filled" (Matthew 5:6). It is not enough to ambitiously yearn to accomplish. According to Jesus, God's Kingdom and His righteousness are the very top priorities in all of life. Seeking God's righteousness is that important.

Our focus should be toward the result. He gives this encouragement and admonishment to motivate us to understand and live all of life in relation to where it ends. Will life end in the Kingdom of God or in the Hell of Fire? That is a choice that each person makes. Even in the everyday, mundane things, eating and drinking, going to work, getting along with others, and so on, God wants His people to relate those daily experiences to their goal, the Kingdom of God.

We know that before a person can achieve good success, he/she must have vision and set the right goal! Jesus clearly established the highest-priority goal for His disciples in this verse. "But seek first the kingdom of God and His righteousness, and all these things shall be added to you." He did this because He knows that the main goal, our highest priority, determines the preparations, efforts, and zeal for reaching it.

In the same chapter we notice what Jesus said earlier in Matthew chapter 6, verses 19 to 21. "Do not lay up for yourselves treasures on earth, where moth and rust destroy and where thieves break in and steal; but lay up for yourselves treasures in heaven, where neither moth nor rust destroys and where thieves do not break in and steal. For where your treasure is, there your heart will be also." Consider these scriptures in the context of what Jesus says in verse 33. Our hearts are in the things to which we devote ourselves, the things we spend our time pursuing. He is helping us prioritize by stating and illustrating principles that will help us make right choices in managing time.

The Power of Connection

But without faith it is impossible to please Him, for he who comes to God must believe that He is, and that He is a rewarder of those who diligently seek Him.

(Hebrews 11:6)

When you connect with faith, it begins to enlarge your capacity to receive. The Word of God says, "Without faith it is impossible to please Him, for he who comes to God must believe that He is, and that He is a rewarder of those who diligently seek Him." Without—Greek, "apart from faith" you cannot see God. To come to God, you must first believe that He is. He is a rewarder of them that seek Him.

How can you obtain or walk in His abundance if you did not believe in Him? But without faith it is impossible to please him – without "confidence" in God – in His fidelity, His truth, His wisdom, and His promises. This is true in matters relating to family issues. It is impossible for a child to please his father unless he has confidence in him. It is

41

impossible for a wife to please her husband, or a husband a wife, unless they have confidence in each other.

He is a rewarder of them that seek Him. That is pursuit connection with faith. When you learn to connect with faith, something begins to well up on the inside of you that gives God the ability to move you in a way that never seemed possible. You begin to get in connection with your destiny that produces the divine abundance.

Believe in the Word of God

Then Elisha said, "Hear the word of the LORD. Thus says the LORD: 'Tomorrow about this time a seah of fine flour shall be sold for a shekel, and two seahs of barley for a shekel, at the gate of Samaria.'" So an officer on whose hand the king leaned answered the man of God and said, "Look, if the LORD would make windows in heaven, could this thing be?" And he said, "In fact, you shall see it with your eyes, but you shall not eat of it."

(2 Kings 7:1-2)

You cannot walk in His divine abundance if you doubt the Word of God. You cannot operate with the spirit of doubt like Thomas and walk in abundance. God had spoken through His prophet, but the king's servant doubted the spoken word of the Man of God. Many times, people walk by sight instead of by faith.

The devastation of the famine was so great that it compelled the king's servant to admit that even God with all His mighty power could not change the situation within twenty-four hours. "Look, if the LORD would make windows in heaven, could this thing be?" And he said, "In fact, you shall see it with your eyes, but you shall not eat of it."

Doubt is a hindrance spirit that prevents people experiencing miracles. God is not limited by doubt or circumstances. God used lepers to bring about that tremendous miracle. Lepers were social outcasts in those days. People disrespected them because leprosy represents sin according to the scriptures. Yet God used them to fulfil His divine purpose for the people of Samaria. Believe in Him that He can turn your affliction, disappointment, lack and shame around for good.

> *Now there were four leprous men at the entrance of the gate; and they said to one another, "Why are we sitting here until we die? If we say, 'We will enter the city,' the famine is in the city, and we shall die there. And if we sit here, we die also. Now therefore, come, let us surrender to the army of the Syrians. If they keep us alive, we shall live; and if they kill us, we shall only die." And they rose at twilight to go to the camp of the Syrians; and when they had come to the outskirts of the Syrian camp, to their surprise no one was there. For the Lord had caused the army of the Syrians to hear the noise of chariots and the noise of horses — the noise of a great army; so they said to one another, "Look, the king of Israel has hired against us the kings of the Hittites and the kings of the Egyptians to attack us!"*
>
> *(2 Kings 7:3-6)*

Is anything too hard for the Lord? NO! "For the Lord had caused the army of the Syrians to hear the noise of chariots and the noise of horses — the noise of a great army; so they said to one another, 'Look, the king of Israel has hired against us the kings of the Hittites and the kings of the Egyptians to attack us!'"

The lepers were not selfish; they did not keep the abundance of the food, clothing, and money they found at the camp of the army of the Syrians for themselves. "Then they said to one another, 'We are not doing right. This day is a day of good news, and we remain silent. If we wait until morning light, some punishment will come upon us. Now therefore, come, let us go and tell the king's household.'

So they went and called to the gatekeepers of the city, and told them, saying, 'We went to the Syrian camp, and surprisingly no one *was* there, not a human sound — only horses and donkeys tied, and the tents intact.' And the gatekeepers called out, and they told *it* to the king's household inside" (2 Kings 7:9-11).

Know that God is the Owner of the Whole World

The scripture makes it clear that God owns everything. The entire world belongs to Him. "The earth *is* the LORD's, and all its fullness, the world and those who dwell therein" (Psalm 24:1). Therefore, the owner laid down clear rules for us by determining the way that we could use for example, His land, money and how to treat His children etc.

He charged the children of Israel that the land had to lie fallow in every seventh year, and only the poor could eat whatever came up then. In every fiftieth year, all slaves had to be set free, all debts cancelled, and all land returned to its original owner. The children of Israel obeyed these rules because they recognized that God was the ultimate owner of all things – He had the right to decide what happened to His property. Accordingly our attitude towards our possessions changes when we deeply acknowledge this truth.

To walk in God's divine provision, we must recognize that we own nothing and that all things belong to God. Our acknowledgement of God's ownership will transform the way we think about giving. Giving must become an integral part of every Christian. God Himself is a giver. Instead of wondering, "How much of my money, time, love, faithfulness, commitment etc., should I give to God?" we ask, "How much of God's money should I keep for myself?"

As stewards, we are called to make our seed or money grow by hard work and careful investment. Walking in God's provision requires diligence and excellence. Sometimes we learn excellence and diligence through pressure. Pressure comes from the word press, which means to suffer hardship or going through difficulty. Life circumstances such as disappointment, rejection and famine, bring suffering into our lives. "Not that I have already attained, or am already perfected; but I **press** on, that I may lay hold of that for which Christ Jesus has also laid hold of me. Brethren, I do not count myself to have apprehended; but one thing *I do*, forgetting those things which are behind and reaching forward to those things which are ahead" (Philippians 3:12-13).

Obedience to God in Crisis

There was a famine in the land, besides the first famine that was in the days of Abraham. And Isaac went to

Abimelech king of the Philistines, in Gerar. Then the LORD appeared to him and said: "Do not go down to Egypt; live in the land of which I shall tell you. Dwell in this land, and I will be with you and bless you; for to you and your descendants I give all these lands, and I will perform the oath which I swore to Abraham your father."

(Genesis 26:1-3)

Crisis is inevitable in the lives of humanity. The above passage of scripture says, there was a famine in the land, besides the first famine that was in the days of Abraham. That means Abraham faced famine and Isaac also went through similar situations. Life will not give you what you want but what you fight for. In this famine God asked Isaac not to go to Egypt as his father, Abraham did and nearly had a problem.

During the famine Isaac sowed in the land. He did not consume all his seed because he was hungry. Going through financial crisis is not advisable to keep what you have, invest or sow. Isaac sowed at the time of famine and reaped one hundred-fold. This proves God's faithfulness in response to Isaac's obedience. God has given us rules of engagement, principles, and keys to open doors of opportunity.

Then Isaac sowed in that land, and reaped in the same year a hundredfold; and the LORD blessed him. The man began to prosper, and continued prospering until he became very prosperous; for he had possessions of flocks and possessions of herds and a great number of servants. So, the Philistines envied him.

(Genesis 26:12-13)

When the Lord asked Isaac not to go to Egypt, He promised him a blessing. But you know something, Isaac did not fold his arms and said, "I am waiting for the Lord's blessing," he worked. Isaac responded by working diligently – sowing seed to preserve his inheritance.

We know that God is our great Provider – *Jehovah Jireh*, but we are to work hard because money comes and increases by hard working and careful investment. God did not promise that He will put money in your bank account, but He promised to provide for our needs. Work diligently and excellently and as you do your strategic moves, God will bless the work of your hands. Then you will walk in His abundance.

❖

CHAPTER 5

God will
Prepare a Table for You

*T*hou preparest a table before me in the presence of mine enemies: thou anointest my head with oil; my cup runneth over. Surely goodness and mercy shall follow me all the days of my life: and I will dwell in the house of the LORD forever.*

(Psalm 23:5-6 KJV)

King David said the Lord is my shepherd. Jesus is the good shepherd who went one step beyond David's list of provision – He gave His life for the sheep. The key to divine provision is the presence of God. The above passage of scripture says, "Thou preparest a table before me" indeed it is the Lord who provides our daily bread.

Surely goodness and mercy shall follow me. The word mercy in Hebrew is *'chesed'* meaning the unfailing, steadfast covenant love of God. He is the giver of all good gifts, and he is our provider. This is a matter for the human heart because, even as Christians, we struggle with economic and financial issues as we learn to depend on God for our supply.

Stop Eating the Crumbs

Covenant members are only allowed to eat from the table of the King. Every believer has the right to partake at the King's table. But many times, some Christians behave like slaves. King David said to Mephibosheth you will eat bread continually at my table based on covenant relationship with David and Jonathan. "And the king called to Ziba, Saul's servant, and said to him, 'I have given to your master's son all that belonged to Saul and to all his house. You, therefore, and your sons and your servants, shall work the land for him, and you shall bring in *the harvest,* that your master's son may have food to eat. But Mephibosheth your master's son shall eat bread at my table always.'

Now Ziba had fifteen sons and twenty servants. Then Ziba said to the king, 'According to all that my lord the king has commanded his servant, so will your servant do.' 'As for Mephibosheth,' said the king, 'he shall eat at my table like one of the king's sons.' Mephibosheth had a young son whose name *was* Micha. And all who dwelt in the house of Ziba *were* servants of Mephibosheth. So, Mephibosheth dwelt in Jerusalem, for he ate continually at the king's table. And he was lame in both his feet" (2 Samuel 9:9-13).

Covenant members or children do not eat the crumbs. David extended an invitation to Jonathan's son, Mephibosheth because of the mutual relationship between himself and Jonathan. Because of the covenant relationship between us and God (through Jesus Christ our Saviour), we have the privilege to receive divine provision from our heavenly Father.

A Gentile woman came to Jesus for help because her daughter was sick. Jesus told this woman that He couldn't give what belongs to the covenant children to dogs (Gentiles). But with the persistent faith of the woman, Jesus permitted her to partake in the table of the covenant children.

And behold, a woman of Canaan came from that region and cried out to Him, saying, "Have mercy on me, O Lord, Son of David! My daughter is severely demon-possessed." But He answered her not a word. And His disciples came and urged Him, saying, "Send her away, for she cries out after us." But He answered and said, "I was not sent except to the lost sheep of the house of Israel." Then she came and worshiped Him, saying, "Lord, help me!" But He answered and said, "It is not good to take the children's bread and throw it to the little dogs." And she said, "Yes, Lord, yet even the little dogs eat the crumbs which fall from their masters' table." Then Jesus answered and said to her, "O woman, great is your faith! Let it be to you as you desire." And her daughter was healed from that very hour.

(Matthew 15:22-28)

As the Gentile woman exercised her faith, so also believers must demonstrate their faith in the Lord by standing on the promises of God, because without faith no one can please God. Christians must have trust in God to receive from Him all our needs according to His riches in Christ Jesus. We belong to the King of kings and therefore, we must stop eating the crumbs.

Scripture warns us against the love of the world. God knows that we have physical and financial needs, but he wants us to get the emphasis right. He wants us to reintroduce into our thinking and understanding an unshakeable confidence that the Lord is God.

We are often driven by anxious thoughts in these troubled times, asking, "How are we going to survive?" Jesus speaks directly into these worries when He says, "Therefore, do not worry, saying, 'What shall we eat?' or 'What shall we drink?' or 'What shall we wear?'"

> Don't worry about anything; instead, pray about everything. Tell God what you need, and thank him for all he has done. Then you will experience God's peace, which exceeds anything we can understand. His peace will guard your hearts and minds as you live in Christ Jesus.
> (Philippians 4:6-7 NLT)

Many Christians today are relentlessly pursuing wealth and happiness within the context of a value system that excludes God. This pursuit shows us the heart of the problem of our society, and I believe it is the result of a misplaced and idolatrous expression of the fundamental needs of the human heart. We are all looking for security, protection, and provision. But we are looking for them in the wrong places. God wants us to depend upon Him only. He said, we should not worry about what we will eat; we should trust Him for our supply of needs.

The Bible says, "For after all these things the Gentiles seek. For your heavenly Father knows that you need all these things. But seek first the kingdom of God and his righteousness and all these things shall be added to you" (Matthew 6:31-33).

Provision comes by putting God first. I know that some people are really struggling and giving presents a very real dilemma for them. But God must come first in your finances. There is no other way to flow in God's provision. If you are in debt, or if you have other financial difficulties to resolve, make sure you honour God first with what you do have.

Prosperity means having the ability to fulfil God's destiny for your life and to bless others in God's plan for them. Jesus gave all He had to us so that we could be rich in all things. "For you know the grace of our Lord Jesus Christ, that though he was rich, yet for your sake he became poor, so that you through his poverty might become rich" (2 Corinthians 8:9 NLT).

As a Christian you cannot walk in God's provision without obedience. Obedience and faithfulness are divine keys to walk in abundance. For example, God says, "Bring all the tithes into the storehouse, that there may be food in my house, and try me now in this," says the LORD of hosts, "If I will not open for you the windows of heaven and pour out for you such blessing that there will not be room enough to receive it" (Malachi 3:10).

The plain fact about God's provision is, the more you give the more you receive! I am not suggesting that you should give with the selfish motive of gaining more yourself. But when you do give you receive back more, and this means that you have even more to give next time. This is the principle of sowing and reaping.

God Wants us to have Confidence in Him

Therefore do not cast away your confidence, which has great reward. For you have need of endurance, so that after you have done the will of God, you may receive the promise: "For yet a little while, And He who is coming will come and will not tarry. Now the just shall live by faith; But if anyone draws back, My soul has no pleasure in him." But we are not of those who draw back to perdition, but of those who believe to the saving of the soul.

(Hebrews 10:35-39)

Every day we hear news globally how many people are losing their jobs, their properties, or assets. Economic worries have become major discussions everywhere, and even though some experts are reporting that the economy may be recovering, almost everyone acknowledges that there is still a long way to go. We must know that if the builder does not build the house the builders build but they will build in vain. Our dependency is of God.

Our current economic situations in many places may be new to us, but famine and financial difficulties are not new. In the Bible we see so many accounts of nations and people who went through economic crisis. The Scripture tells the story of a widow whose husband had died, leaving her with the burden of his unpaid debts. Not only that, but the creditor was threatening to take her two sons into slavery to pay the debts.

The widow had limited resources and faced an impossible situation. She did the only thing she knew to do. She cried out for help. She went to Elisha, the prophet of God, and told him of her situation. Elisha asked her a crucial question: "What do you have in your house?" The widow replied that she had nothing but a little oil. She probably thought this small thing was of no consequence compared to the enormous problem she faced. However, God had a plan to use what the widow had.

Elisha instructed her to borrow jars from her neighbours and to fill each jar with her oil. The widow followed his instructions, and a miracle occurred. The little amount of oil she had continued to fill each jar until there were no empty jars left. The widow was then able to sell the oil to others and gain income to pay her husband's creditor. There was even enough money left for the widow and her sons to live on.

Now there cried a certain woman of the wives of the sons of the prophets unto Elisha, saying, Thy servant my husband is dead; and thou knowest that thy servant did fear the Lord: and the creditor is come to take unto him my two sons to be bondmen. And Elisha said unto her, what shall I do for thee? tell me, what hast thou in the house? And she said, Thine handmaid hath not any thing in the house, save a pot of oil. Then he said, Go, borrow thee vessels abroad of all thy neighbours, even empty vessels; borrow not a few. And when thou art come in, thou shalt shut the door upon thee and upon thy sons, and shalt pour out into all those vessels, and thou shalt set aside that which is full. So she went from him, and shut the door upon her and upon her sons, who brought the vessels to her; and she poured out. And it came to pass, when the vessels were full, that she said unto her son, Bring me yet a vessel. And he said unto her, There is not a vessel more. And the oil stayed. Then she came and told the man of God. And he said, Go, sell the oil, and pay thy debt, and live thou and thy children of the rest.

(1 Kings 4:1-7 KJV)

God wants us to trust in His provision for our needs, and sometimes that provision requires us to step out in faith and use what resources He has given us. It may not seem like a lot to us, but God can multiply the efforts when we trust Him. How can you apply this story today?

First, acknowledge God's Lordship of your life. Cry out to Him with your needs. Also, be willing to let others know of your need. Perhaps God wants to bless both you and them by allowing them to provide for a need, but they cannot if you will not let your need be known.

What do you have that God can use? Perhaps you have a possession that can be sold to pay off debts, or perhaps the possession is the debt, as in an expensive car or home. Selling that possession and downsizing to something more affordable could make you debt free. If you are facing what seems like an impossible situation, pray about your needs. Ask God to show you His plan for your provision and be open to letting others know about your needs.

Ask God to give you insights on how you can use what He has already given you in a new way. Perhaps you are not in need right now, but you have extra resources that could help someone else. Ask God to put someone on your heart who needs your help. He may have gifted you with this resource for the specific purpose of providing for someone else; what a blessing it would be, if you could use God's resources for His purposes.

The Lord Gives us Power to Walk in Abundance

You may say to yourself, "My power and the strength of my hands have produced this wealth for me." But remember the LORD your God, for it is he who gives you the ability to produce wealth, and so confirms his covenant, which he swore to your ancestors, as it is today.
(Deuteronomy 8:17-18 NIV)

The Word of God states clearly that one of the blessings that God has ordained for us is to be so supernaturally provided for - that we have more than enough of everything! Not just for ourselves - but so that we have more than enough to bless others when they need it!

If you walk in obedience to God, you will not only experience the supernatural provisions of the Lord, but you will also have more than enough. In the book of Deuteronomy Chapter 28, we see the promises of God concerning obedience and blessings. Unless we willfully *reject* what God has said - we cannot read these verses and not see that God wants us to have not simply enough to get by on - but so much that we put fear into others because they recognize that it is the

Living God whom we serve - and it causes them to turn to Him as well! "The blessing of the LORD, it maketh rich, and he addeth no sorrow with it" (Proverbs 10:22 KJV).

The Word of God teaches repeatedly that *Godly* prosperity is not only a blessing from God - but necessary to the Christian to fulfil the plan of God on this earth through the body of Christ, just as God blessed Abraham to become a channel of blessing to many generations. God made him extraordinarily rich in material goods – silver and cattle that are money. According to the Word of God, He was supernaturally blessed.

Be Diligent about your Work

The Bible says, "Whatever your hand finds to do, do *it* with you might; for *there is* no work or device or knowledge or wisdom in the grave where you are going" (Ecclesiastes 9:10). Commitment and hard work can bring you out of poverty. God wants people to be serious about their work. Laziness would lead to lack. Laziness can lead to stealing. "Let him that stole steal no more: but rather let him labour, working with his hands the thing, which is good, that he may have to give to him that needs it" (Ephesians 4:28).

To become more successful in life learn new things or acquire more knowledge of the field of your carrier. "A house is built by wisdom and becomes strong through good sense. Through knowledge its rooms are filled with all sorts of precious riches and valuables" (Proverbs 24:3-4).

Through the redemption of our Lord Jesus Christ, you can walk in God's divine provision. Through obedience, faith, confidence, faithfulness you can walk in abundance. "Christ has redeemed us from the curse of the law, having become a curse for us (for it is written, 'Cursed *is* everyone who hangs on a tree'), that the blessing of Abraham might come upon the Gentiles in Christ Jesus, that we might receive the promise of the Spirit through faith" (Galatians 3:13-14).

Trust the Lord with All Your heart

Trust in the LORD *and do good; dwell in the land and enjoy safe pasture. Take delight in the* LORD, *and he will give you the desires of your heart.*

(Psalm 37:3-4 NIV)

Our greatest downfall in life is that we fail to trust God. Our heart, (that is our intellect, inner person or deepest thoughts), sometimes deceive us that God does not care for us. But God cares for us. King David said, "I have been young, and now am old; yet I have not seen the righteous forsaken, nor his descendants begging bread. He is ever merciful, and lends, and his descendants are blessed" (Psalm 37:25-26). The righteous are always protected by God. "I have not seen the righteous forsaken, nor his descendants begging bread."

The primary thought of this psalm is trust in God to bring about economic in His time. Humankind should not depend upon their own wisdom and understanding, in the conduct of civil life, but should seek the direction and blessing of providence, or otherwise will meet with disappointment; and, when they succeed, should ascribe it not to their own prudence and wisdom, but to the goodness of God.

Without reliance on or confidence in God, it is impossible to carry out any of the precepts of the Word of God. *"Batakh"* is, properly, "to cling to," and so passes to the meaning of "to confide in," "to set one's hope and confidence upon." "The wicked run away when no one is chasing them, but the godly are as bold as lions" (Proverbs 28:1). Confidence gives boldness, *"Trust in the Lord with all thy heart"* — wholly and securely relies upon God's wisdom, power, and goodness, and upon his providence and promises, we are to trust Him for direction and help in all manners and affairs.

> *Trust in the LORD with all thine heart; and lean not unto thine own understanding.*
>
> *(Proverbs 3:5 KJV)*

> *It is better to trust in the LORD than to put confidence in man. It is better to trust in the LORD than to put confidence in princes.*
>
> *(Psalm 118:8-9 KJV)*

I suppose this passage of scripture, "It is better to trust in the LORD than to put confidence in man," is the centre of the Bible. If mankind will learn to trust and have confidence in God many of our problems, we face in life would be over. God wishes us all the best in life. Our heavenly Father desires that we will live in abundance. "The thief does not come except to steal, and to kill, and to destroy. I have come that they may have life, and that they may have it more abundantly" (John 10:10).

The word abundantly in Greek is *"perissos"* meaning superabundance, excessive, overflowing, surplus, over, and above, more than enough, extraordinary, above the ordinary, more than enough. God desires divine abundance for you. As you give your entire self to Him, He will give His total self to you.

Jesus said that He came to give life – not just ordinary existence, but life in fullness, copious, and prosperity. On the other hand, the enemy, Satan comes only to steal, kill, and destroy. Friend, you know the line is clearly drawn, on one side is God with goodness, life, and plenty of all that is necessary for life, and on the other side is the devil of souls, who comes to rob us of our Lord's blessings. Jesus, who is a good shepherd, provides the sheep, (us) with abundant life and provision.

A Seed to the Sower

Now may He who supplies seed to the sower, and bread for food, supply and multiply the seed you have sown and increase the fruits of your righteousness, while you are enriched in everything for all liberality, which causes thanksgiving through us to God.
(2 Corinthians 9:10-11)

God is the One who supplies seed to us. Seed are not meant for consumption but rather to plant. The purpose of planting the seed is to insert increase. The God who gave you seed in the first place is the One who meets your basic needs, multiplies your seed sown into abundance so that you can share your harvest with others.

God is the One who makes all grace abound towards us and provides us sufficiency in all things. All things beneficial for our lives come from God's hands. We are given sufficiency even "extraordinary" so that we might do good work. We are blessed to be a blessing to others as God said to Abraham, "I will make you a great nation; I will bless you and make your name great; **And you shall be a blessing**" (Genesis 12:2).

Generous giving meets the material needs of others but also produces many thanksgivings to God. Any time you provide for someone's needs you are creating and atmosphere for global thanksgiving to God. You know what? The person would thank you and gives thanks to God for meeting their needs and this will course much thanksgiving globally to God. God deserves our gratitude. The more you give the more you will be blessed. God loves a cheerful giver.

A cheerful giver describes a person who has a spirit of enjoyment in giving that sweeps away all restraints. The joy of giving is greater and stronger than the blessing of giving. God gives to us without receiving any blessing from us, but the joy of giving compels Him to give to us all the time. He is a good and loving Father.

> But this I say: He who sows sparingly will also reap sparingly, and he who sows bountifully will also reap bountifully. So let each one give as he purposes in his heart, not grudgingly or of necessity; for God loves a cheerful giver. And God is able to make all grace abound toward you, that you, always having all sufficiency in all things, may have an abundance for every good work. As it is written: "He has dispersed abroad, He has given to the poor; His righteousness endures forever."
>
> (2 Corinthians 9:6-9)

The Miracle Seed

Everything you have today came as result of a seed. Whenever you sell your seed, you are sacrificing your future for the present. We do not sell our seed, we sow it, and then our seed works for us in famine. One of the reasons some parts of the world have been on the brink of disaster because of famine is because people eat their seed instead of sowing it.

"Now there was a famine in the land—besides the previous famine in Abraham's time—and Isaac went to Abimelek king of the Philistines in Gerar. The LORD appeared to Isaac and said, 'Do not go down to Egypt; live in the land where I tell you to live. Stay in this land for a while, and I will be with you and will bless you. For to you and your descendants I will give all these lands and will confirm the oath I swore to your father Abraham'" (Genesis 26:1-3 NIV).

If a person keeps seeds in his hand he will starve, but the moment he put them into the ground, God gives him a hundredfold.

Then Isaac sowed in that land, and received in the same year an hundredfold: and the Lord blessed him. And the man waxed great, and went forward, and grew until he became very great: For he had possession of flocks, and possession of herds, and great store of servants: and the Philistines envied him.

(Genesis 26:12-14 KJV)

Every child of God does not just possess the seed of God; they have become that seed. They are a seed because they are a child of God. Whenever a seed dies, it brings forth more seed. That is why God said that He would see His seed, implying that after Jesus Christ died, He would resurrect. Jesus, the Seed of the Kingdom, died and out of Him came much seed, which includes you and me. That is the reason why whatsoever we do in His name, we procreate that seed of God in the earth.

> *Verily, verily, I say unto you, Except a corn of wheat fall into the ground and die, it abideth alone: but if it die, it bringeth forth much fruit.*
>
> *(John 12:24 KJV)*

In the book of Zechariah 8:12 it says, "For the seed shall be prosperous; the vine shall give her fruit, and the ground shall give her increase, and the heavens shall give their dew; and I will cause the **remnant of this people** to possess all these things." The term remnant of this people refers to the seed or the fruit that had remained. The seed helps us proper because it carries within itself the ability to prosper. When you have no seed there is no prosperity.

So, friend, do not misuse your seed, there is no other way you would prosper without seed. Therefore, what God gives us is seed and that seed shall prosper. Prosperity comes by the way of the seed-principle, for in one seed there is such great potential. The grace, love, faith, kindness, anointing, unity, goodness etc., that are upon our lives will increase all the time if it is treated as a seed. The widow who had a little oil in a jar, which the prophet Elisha instructed to borrow vessels, not a few and pour the little oil she had, was a seed. God always wants us to trust Him with our seed for increase.

Whenever we plant it, prosperity will come and increase will be ours.

Running on Empty to Fullness

A certain woman of the wives of the sons of the prophets cried out to Elisha, saying, "Your servant my husband is dead, and you know that your servant feared the LORD. And the creditor is coming to take my two sons to be his slaves." So Elisha said to her, "What shall I do for you? Tell me, what do you have in the house?" And she said, "Your maidservant has nothing in the house but a jar of oil."

Then he said, "Go, borrow vessels from everywhere, from all your neighbours – empty vessels; do not gather just a few. And when you have come in, you shall shut the door behind you and your sons; then pour it into all those vessels, and set aside the full ones." So she went from him and shut the door behind her and her sons, who brought the vessels to her; and she poured it out. Now it came to pass, when the vessels were full, that she said to her son, "Bring me another vessel." And he said to her, "There is not another vessel." So the oil ceased. Then she came and told the man of God. And he said, "Go, sell the oil and pay your debt; and you and your sons live on the rest."

(2 Kings 4:1-7)

Do you know that emptiness can be a wonderful gift and opportunity? Emptiness is a gift from the Lord; those who are hungry or thirsty shall be filled. The destitute widow learned a great lesson from the prophet of God – Elisha. God have enough to provide for all those who are empty and hunger for God's divine supply. Emptiness tells us that we have a need. One day the prophet Elisha meets a woman with nothing – no husband, no income, no food, no prospects and was in indebt. We must admit our emptiness and believe that only God can truly fill us.

When Elisha asked the woman "what do you have in the house?" She replied, "A jar of oil" *(or a jar of almost empty oil!)* Friend, if you are full, you cannot be filled. Emptiness is not a disgrace it is a blessing. The prophet tells her to gather what she has and returns with a jar of oil and several empty jars from neighbours. She then begins to pour her oil into the empty jars, and she just keeps on pouring until all the jars are full. Only then does the oil in the first jar run out.

Interestingly, God's provision has no limit; the woman gets as much oil, as she has empty jars. There is something about "emptiness" or "nothing" that moves God's hand. He loves leading us to empty places where we can lean on nothing except His provision, could it be that we are not empty enough? Could we still be distracted and dependent on ourselves? This story teaches us that emptiness is a gift from God. Elisha did not only meet the widow's present needs but also her long-range ones as well.

Remember, anytime you are full, the oil will cease. We must empty ourselves for the Holy Spirit of God to fill us with fresh oil. **"Now it came to pass, when the vessels were full, that she said to her son, 'Bring me another vessel.' And he said to her, 'There is not another vessel.' So the oil ceased"** (2 Kings 4:6).

❖

CHAPTER 6

Understanding of
Open and Closed Heavens

*A*nd your heavens which are over your head shall
*be bronze, and the earth which is under you shall
be iron. The* LORD *will change the rain of your
land to powder and dust; from the heaven it shall come
down on you until you are destroyed.*

(Deuteronomy 28:23-24)

What happens when the heavens are closed? We see
through the Bible with numerous instances that caused the
heavens to be closed. Disobedience, sin, curses and all kinds
of evil are some of the reasons that heavens can be closed.
God charged the children of Israel that if they disobeyed
Him their heavens would be closed and likewise if they obey,
heaven will then be opened for His divine blessings.

"But it shall come to pass, if you do not obey the voice of the LORD your God, to observe carefully all His commandments and His statutes which I command you today, that all these curses will come upon you and overtake you: Cursed shall you be in the city, and cursed shall you be in the country. Cursed shall be your basket and your kneading bowl. Cursed shall be the fruit of your body and the produce of your land, the increase of your cattle and the offspring of your flocks. Cursed shall you be when you come in and cursed shall you be when you go out" (Deuteronomy 28:15-19).

Your Heaven

The Bible talks about your heaven – that means, every person has a geographical area over their head called "YOUR HEAVEN." Your breakthrough in life depends upon the kind of heaven you are under. For example, two people can live in the same area, in a family or in a city but one be living a prosperous life, while the other struggling and walking in defeat and failure. "And your heavens which are over your head shall be bronze, and the earth which is under you shall be iron."

Friend, do you know something? The earth is a product of heaven. The earth cannot be fruitful without heaven's influence. The earth cannot produce crops without heaven giving rain. "Before any plant of the field was in the earth and before any herb of the field had grown. For the LORD God had not caused it to rain on the earth, and *there was* no man to till the ground" (Genesis 2:5). God is the One who causes the heavens to influence the earth. "Every good thing given and every perfect gift is from above, coming down from the

68

Father of lights, with whom there is no variation or shifting shadow" (James 1:17 NASB).

So, when your heaven is closed, it affects your earth. "And your heavens which are over your head shall be bronze, and the **earth which is under you shall be iron.** The LORD will change the rain of your land to powder and dust; from the heaven it shall come down on you until you are destroyed." When your earth becomes like iron whatever you sow will die and you will become unproductive. Evil, sin and disobedience are the doors to close heaven and earth. "The LORD will send on you cursing, confusion, and rebuke in all that you set your hand to do, until you are destroyed and until you perish quickly, because of the wickedness of your doings in which you have forsaken Me. The LORD will make the plague cling to you until He has consumed you from the land which you are going to possess" (Deuteronomy 28:20-21).

When the heavens over your head become bronze, and the earth, which is under you becomes iron, you can face a severe famine. We have many people going through devastation in the world we live in because of disobedience to God. Nations or families can go through closing heaven and earth due to disobedience and evil. "Your sons and your daughters *shall be* given to another people, and your eyes shall look and fail *with longing* for them all day long; and *there shall* be no strength in your hand. A nation whom you have not known shall eat the fruit of your land and the produce of your labour, and you shall be only oppressed and crushed continually" (Deuteronomy 28:32-33).

Under closed heavens, demonic activity becomes quite rampant, in one's life and endeavours. The Word of God teaches us that demons search for dry places – emptiness and the vacuum left by the departure of an evil spirit must be filled with the Holy Spirit or else the person is open to the demonic. You must ask, are my heavens opened or closed? Am I really concerned about my life, calling, purpose, divine gratuity and destiny?

Under closed heavens, everything will be hard for you. Prayer becomes so difficult, and demons overcome you. Under closed heavens:

- You will invest much but reap little

- You will sweat much but have little to show for your great efforts

- Demon devourers are released unto one's labour or work

The inevitability of these curses would be real for believers today, were it not removed by Jesus Christ who has redeemed us from the curse of the law, having become a curse for us. We must walk in obedience and truth because the wrath of God is revealed from heaven against the disobedience and unrighteousness of men. "Now it shall come to pass, if you diligently obey the voice of the LORD your God, to observe carefully all His commandments which I command you today, that the LORD your God will set you high above all nations of the earth" (Deuteronomy 28:1).

Repentance Releases God's Mercy

When we spend time in repentance for our sins and our land and extend our prayers to include geographical areas like our country, neighbourhood, family, home, business, church, and ministry, God will forgive and heal us. Prayer and fasting are supernatural tools to reach God for mercy. The prophet Joel prophesied at a time of great devastation to the entire land of Judah. An enormous plague of locusts had denuded the countryside of all vegetation, destroyed the pastures of both the sheep and the cattle, and even stripped the bark off the fig trees.

The plague of locusts the prophet wrote about was greater than anyone had ever seen. All crops were lost and the seed crops for next planting were destroyed. A famine and drought had seized the entire land. Both people and animals were dying. In fact, it was so profound and disastrous that Joel saw only one explanation; it was the judgment of God. He therefore advised the children of Israel to seek the face of God for help with fasting and prayer. "Consecrate a fast, call a sacred assembly; Gather the elders *and* all the inhabitants of the land *into* the house of the LORD your God, And cry out to the LORD" (Joel 1:14).

> *Therefore also now, saith the LORD, turn ye even to me with all your heart, and with fasting, and with weeping, and with mourning: And rend your heart, and not your garments, and turn unto the LORD your God: for he is gracious and merciful, slow to anger, and of great kindness, and repenteth him of the evil. Who knoweth if he will return and repent, and leave a blessing behind him;*

even a meat offering and a drink offering unto the LORD *your God?*

Blow the trumpet in Zion, sanctify a fast, call a solemn assembly: Gather the people, sanctify the congregation, assemble the elders, gather the children, and those that suck the breasts: let the bridegroom go forth of his chamber, and the bride out of her closet. Let the priests, the ministers of the LORD, *weep between the porch and the altar, and let them say, Spare thy people, O* LORD, *and give not thine heritage to reproach, that the heathen should rule over them: wherefore should they say among the people, Where is their God?*

(Joel 2:12-17 KJV)

The destruction comes through a locust invasion, a drought and famine and fire. This question, addressed to the leaders and the children of Israel, is designed to show that this is no mere natural calamity, but in fact, a judgment of the Lord. When we are dealing with God, we are never without hope. Even amid extreme circumstances, which, as in this case, are His judgments, we can turn our hearts to Him and find help and salvation. He is never vindictive or cruel. Rather, He is gracious and merciful, slow to anger, and of great kindness.

Rend your heart, and not your garments – the tearing of one's garment was a common practice in times of grief or contrition. It symbolized a broken and torn spirit. Here the prophet Joel is calling Judah to experience what this symbolism portrays: hearts that are torn with grief and confession of their sins. God is calling Christians to render their hearts not their garments for repentance and forgiveness of sin to others. We should show the same mercy and kindness to our fellow brethren who have offended us.

In God's message of judgment always has the intent of repentance and reconciliation. Nineveh's repentance releases God's mercy – God changed His mind.

> *So the people of Nineveh believed God, and proclaimed a fast, and put on sackcloth, from the greatest of them even to the least of them. For word came unto the king of Nineveh, and he arose from his throne, and he laid his robe from him, and covered him with sackcloth, and sat in ashes. And he caused it to be proclaimed and published through Nineveh by the decree of the king and his nobles, saying, Let neither man nor beast, herd nor flock, taste any thing: let them not feed, nor drink water: But let man and beast be covered with sackcloth, and cry mightily unto God: yea, let them turn everyone from his evil way, and from the violence that is in their hands. Who can tell if God will turn and repent, and turn away from his fierce anger, that we perish not? And God saw their works, that they turned from their evil way; and God repented of the evil, that he had said that he would do unto them; and he did it not.*
>
> *(Jonah 3:5-10 KJV)*

What Happens when Heaven is Opened?

The issue of an open heaven is very crucial in our pursuit of excellence in life and calling because God does not guide or speak to people living under a closed heaven. "When He had been baptized, Jesus came up immediately from the water; and behold, the heavens were opened to Him, and He saw the Spirit of God descending like a dove and alighting upon Him. And suddenly a voice *came* from heaven, saying, 'This is My beloved Son, in whom I am well pleased'" (Matthew 3:16-17). For your destiny, life and purpose to prosper, the heavens must be involved, because the earth is the product of heaven.

The Spirit anointed Jesus Christ for His ministry. The dove symbolized gentleness, innocence, and meekness, and it was offered in sacrifice, see Leviticus 12:6. Jesus, the obedient Child of God was baptized, and heaven opened for Him to hear the voice of the Father. Obedience is a key to an open heaven for every child of God.

Your destiny will remain stagnant until a connection is made between heaven and earth. When your heavens are opened, your spiritual ladder will be located.

When he reached a certain place, he stopped for the night because the sun had set. Taking one of the stones there, he put it under his head and lay down to sleep. He had a dream in which he saw a stairway resting on the earth, with its top reaching to heaven, and the angels of God were ascending and descending on it.

There above it stood the LORD, and he said: "I am the LORD, the God of your father Abraham and the God of Isaac. I will give you and your descendants the land on which you are lying. Your descendants will be like the dust of the earth, and you will spread out to the west and

to the east, to the north and to the south. All peoples on
earth will be blessed through you and your offspring. I am
with you and will watch over you wherever you go, and I
will bring you back to this land. I will not leave you until
I have done what I have promised you."

(Genesis 28:11-15 NIV)

Jacob's dream emphasizes God's initiating grace as He assures him, He is the Lord of the past and future. Jacob was the third generation to receive the promises of the Abrahamic covenant. Since Jacob had probably never heard God's voice before, the Lord identified Himself by His prior relationship with Abraham and Isaac. Jacob associated God with the place where he had the dream. He memorialized it with the stone at his head and consecrated it with oil.

When the heavens are opened, God will direct and guide you to green pastures and be actively engaged in your affairs. We must make sure our prayer, fasting, giving and our ministry to God and men are all done under an open heaven.

Until your heavens are opened over your head spiritually, your destiny is as good as dead. Cain lived under a closed heaven and confessed, "My punishment *is* greater than I can bear!" "'So now you *are* cursed from the earth, which has opened its mouth to receive your brother's blood from your hand. When you till the ground, it shall no longer yield its strength to you. A fugitive and a vagabond you shall be on the earth.' And Cain said to the LORD, 'My punishment *is* greater than I can bear! Surely You have driven me out this day from the face of the ground; I shall be hidden from Your face; I shall be a fugitive and a vagabond on the earth, and it will happen *that* anyone who finds me will kill me'" (Genesis 4:11-14).

God pronounced a curse upon Cain, "When you till the ground, it shall no longer yield its strength to you." The earth became like iron for Cain. Symbolically, iron and brass in the spirit mean: famine, profitless labour, setbacks, suppression, bondage, failure, and demonic oppression.

It is my sincere desire and prayer that we all operate under an open heaven. As Jacob had a revelation of God – he saw a connection between heaven and earth. He saw a ladder (or stairway) erected on the earth with the top reaching to heaven. Every time the heavens are open, there will always be a connection between heaven and earth.

Jacob understood by revelation, that an access – a gateway to the very throne of God had been opened to him. That is what happens when the heavens become open unto us. God's promise to Jacob was a promise of divine inheritance, fruitfulness, multiplication and expansion, honour and influence, God's presence, protection, direction, and guidance. It is my ardent desire that we all operate under open heavens with obedience to receive blessings and divine protection from God. "Oh, that you would rend (open) the heavens and come down, that the mountains would tremble before you! As when fire sets twigs ablaze and causes water to boil, come down to make your name known to your enemies and cause the nations to quake (or Shake) before you!" (Isaiah 61:1-2 NIV)

To Maintain God's Divine Blessing you must Be Rich Towards God

One of the purposes of God's blessing us, is that we will be a blessing to others. God never intended that we would become selfish. He said to Abraham. I will bless you so that you become a blessing to others. God hates greed and covetousness. We must all become rich towards God by thinking about others and be mindful about the kingdom of God. Our life in heaven is more important than in earth. Jesus said, we should take heed and beware of covetousness, for one's life does not consist in the abundance of the things one possesses.

> Then one from the crowd said to Him, "Teacher, tell my brother to divide the inheritance with me." But He said to him, "Man, who made Me a judge or an arbitrator over you?" And He said to them, "Take heed and beware of covetousness, for one's life does not consist in the abundance of the things he possesses." Then He spoke a parable to them, saying: "The ground of a certain rich man yielded plentifully. And he thought within himself, saying, 'What shall I do, since I have no room to store my crops?' So he said, 'I will do this: I will pull down my barns and build greater, and there I will store all my crops and my goods. And I will say to my soul, Soul, you have many goods laid up for many years; take your ease; eat, drink, and be merry.' But God said to him, 'Fool! This night your soul will be required of you; then whose will those things be which you have provided?' "So is he who lays up treasure for himself, and is not rich toward God."
> (Luke 12:13-21)

Why is the Rich Farmer called a Fool?

One could easily argue that the rich man is a wise and responsible person. He has a thriving or prosperous farming business. His land has produced so abundantly that he does not have enough storage space in his barns or warehouse. So, he plans to pull down his barns and build bigger ones to store all his grain and goods.

Then he will have ample savings set aside for the future and will be all set to enjoy his golden years. Is not this what we are encouraged to strive for? Isn't it wise and responsible to save for the future? The rich farmer would probably be a **good financial advisor**. He seems to have things figured out. He has worked hard and saved wisely. Now he can sit back, relax, and enjoy the fruits of his labour, right? He applied the law of expansion.

What is expansion? To expand something is to increase the extent of it. It is to increase the number or scope of that thing. The word expansion also means to feel generous or optimistic. To be optimistic is to have a high spirit and positive outlook. You cannot expand your business if you do not have a positive outlook about it. Optimism and enthusiasm are godly characteristics. Consequently, they are also a powerful spiritual force. If this businessman has all these qualities, why should Jesus say he is a fool?

There is one particularly important thing the rich man has not planned for - his reckoning with God, his relationship with God. The man has no plan for the kingdom of God. He had not thought of his life after this physical world. But God said to him, "'You fool! This night your soul will be required of you; then whose will those things be which you have provided?' 'So *is* he who lays up treasure for himself and is not rich toward God.'"

The rich farmer is a fool not because he is wealthy or because he saves for the future, but because he appears to live only for himself, and because he believes that he can secure his life with his abundant possessions. When the rich man talks in this parable, he talks only to himself, and the only person he refers to is himself:

"And he thought within himself, saying, 'What shall I do, since I have no room to store my crops?' So he said, 'I will do this: I will pull down my barns and build greater, and there I will store all my crops and my goods.' And I will say to my soul, 'Soul, you have many goods laid up for many years; take your ease; eat, drink, *and* be merry.' But God said to him, 'Fool! This night your soul will be required of you; then whose will those things be which you have provided?' 'So *is* he who lays up treasure for himself and is not rich toward God'" (Luke 12:17-19).

The rich man's land has produced abundantly, yet he expresses no sense of gratitude to God or to the workers who have helped him plant and harvest this bumper crop. He has more grain and goods in storage than he could ever hope to use yet seems to have no thought of sharing it with others, and no thought of what God might require of him. He is blind to the fact that his life is not his own to secure, that his life belongs to God, and that God can demand it back at any time.

All that we work so hard for in life will end up in someone else's hands, and as Ecclesiastes puts it, "Who knows whether they will be wise or foolish? Yet they will be master of all for which I toiled and used my wisdom under the sun. This also is vanity" (Ecclesiastes 2:19).

There are so many people who are enticed by materialism. Our reality is that no matter how much we have, we are always aware of things we do not have. Like the rich farmer, we are tempted to think that having large amounts of money and possessions stored up will make us secure. Sooner or later, however, we learn that no amount of wealth or property can secure our lives. No amount of wealth can protect us from danger, disease or from a tragic accident. No amount of wealth can keep our relationships healthy and our families from falling apart.

In fact, wealth and property can easily drive a wedge between family members, as in the case of the brothers fighting over their inheritance at the beginning of this text. Most importantly, no amount of wealth can secure our lives with God. Jesus said to them, "Take heed! And beware of covetousness (greed), for one's life does not consist in the abundance of things he possesses" (Luke 12:15).

It is not that God does not want us to save for retirement or future needs. It is not that God does not want us to "eat, drink, and be merry" and enjoy what God has given us. We know from the Gospels that Jesus spent time eating and drinking with people and enjoying life. But he was also clear about where his true security lay. It is all about priorities. It is about who is truly God in our lives. It is about how we invest our lives and the gifts that God has given us.

It is about how our lives are fundamentally aligned: toward our passing desires, and ourselves or toward God and our neighbours, toward God's mission to bless and redeem the world. Our lives and possessions are not our own. They belong to God. We are merely stewards of them for the time God has given us on this earth. "Now godliness with contentment is great gain. For we brought nothing into *this* world, *and it is* certain we can carry nothing out. And having food and clothing, with these we shall be content. But those who desire to be rich fall into temptation and a snare, and *into* many foolish and harmful lusts which drown men in destruction and perdition. For the love of money is a root of all *kinds of* evil, for which some have strayed from the faith in their greediness and pierced themselves through with many sorrows" (1 Timothy 6:6-10).

God wants us to walk in His divine prosperity, blessed and being great in this world but most importantly, He wants us to be rich towards heaven our permanent home where death, sorrow, pain, and weeping is no more. Our lives are more important than the wealth of this world, "for one's life does not consist in the abundance of the things he possesses."

Treasure in Heaven

God desires that we walk in His divine provision so that we can build up treasure not only on earth but also in heaven. Our earthly prosperity must reflect in heaven. In other words, our heats must be in heaven because heaven is our final and eternal home. "Lay not up for yourselves treasures upon earth, where moth and rust doth corrupt, and where thieves break through and steal: But lay up for yourselves treasures in heaven, where neither moth nor rust doth corrupt, and where thieves do not break through nor steal: For where your treasure is, there will your heart be also" (Matthew 6:19-21 KJV).

God's desire for us on planet earth is that we prosper. "Beloved, I wish above all things that thou mayest prosper and be in health, even as thy soul prospereth" (3 John 1:2 KJV). He wants us to have our basic needs here, but most importantly, He desires for us to build treasure in heaven.

In the book, "Kingdom Principles" the writer states that, "Now God could, by the sovereign act of creation, not only creates the materials but likewise erects the facility. God has not chosen to work unilaterally. He works with loving, willing, cooperative people. He doesn't need our money and yet He does because He has chosen to bless us (which He always wants to) as we willingly bless Him. Because people fail to recognize this, we give as a reluctant child hesitates to part with its pennies that were initially placed in them by the parent. Giving to God is only returning that which was initially given to us" (Alex W. Ness, p. 266).

When it comes to giving, we cannot discriminate with God because all things belong to Him. If our heart is in heavenly things, it will be evidenced when we invest in heavenly things. We must however, balance our remarks with the legitimacy of possessing material things. The danger must be stressed in not allowing material things to possess us. God allows man to own land and houses and money that are legitimately acquired. God gave Israel land, blessed, and replenished their cattle. He has promised to bless and increase the bounty of those who faithfully serve Him. God takes no delight in the poverty of His creatures no more than we would delight in the poverty of our children. Care must be taken not to be so absorbed with possessions that we neglect or forget the Giver of all things. Because you know something, all our possessions on earth are subject to deterioration and theft.

In conclusion, why are true riches called treasure? Jesus talks about the treasure in the field. The wise sold all they had to buy the field with the treasure. Until we make such a discovery and proceed to acquire it, we are like the church of the Laodiceans who said, "we are rich and increased with goods," but were diagnosed as poor and wretched. "Because you say, 'I am rich, have become wealthy, and have need of nothing' — and do not know that you are wretched, miserable, poor, blind, and naked — I counsel you to buy from Me gold refined in the fire, that you may be rich; and white garments, that you may be clothed, *that* the shame of your nakedness may not be revealed; and anoint your eyes with eye salve, that you may see" (Revelation 3:17-18).

Be Generous to Those Who Are in Need

People who serve the true God have been released by Him from their slavery to mammon, and they show this by giving with God's generosity and compassion. Such people will have treasure in heaven. But remember, generous giving does not save us, it shows that we have been saved.

Jesus' teaching on giving comes in His Sermon on the Mount. "Give to him who asks you, and from him who wants to borrow from you do not turn away" (Matthew 5:42). In the middle of the Sermon on the Mount, that wonderful collection of kingdom principles – Jesus orders this. "Lay not up for yourselves treasures upon earth, where moth and rust doth corrupt, and where thieves break through and steal: But lay up for yourselves treasures in heaven, where neither moth nor rust doth corrupt, and where thieves do not break through nor steal: For where your treasure is, there will your heart be also" (Matthew 6:19-21 KJV).

Be Generous to God

Everything mankind has belongs to God. We own nothing in this world. God blesses us so that we can also finance His kingdom work. In the book, "Giving and Receiving," the writer states, "How did Jesus survive financially? He travelled constantly in Israel after He stopped working as a carpenter – much of the time with the twelve apostles. They needed food to eat and somewhere to sleep. But who gave so that Jesus could train His disciples, teach the crowds, and heal the sick? The gospels are full of instances when people provided Jesus and the twelve with hospitality" (Morris Cerullo, p. 80).

We see from the scriptures that Mary, Martha, and Lazarus provided for Jesus' ministry. "Now it happened as they went that He entered a certain village; and a certain woman named Martha welcomed Him into her house. And she had a sister called Mary, who also sat at Jesus' feet and heard His word. But Martha was distracted with much serving, and she approached Him and said, 'Lord, do You not care that my sister has left me to serve alone? Therefore, tell her to help me.' And Jesus answered and said to her, 'Martha, Martha, you are worried and troubled about many things. But one thing is needed, and Mary has chosen that good part, which will not be taken away from her'" (Luke 10:38-42). To walk in God's divine prosperity, we must be generous to all those are in need and support the Great Commission.

❖

CHAPTER 7

The Great Transfer of Wealth

A good man leaves an inheritance to his children's children, But the wealth of the sinner is stored up for the righteous.

(Proverbs 13:22)

Friends, this wonderful promise reveals the heart of God and His love for His children. The Lord wants to bless us with the wealth of the world for a reason. First and foremost, the scripture says, "The earth is the LORD's, and the fulness thereof; the world, and they that dwell therein" (Psalm 24:1 KJV). Since the earth and everything in it belongs to God, He will give it to His children.

For the LORD God is a sun and shield; The LORD will give grace and glory; No good thing will He withhold from those who walk uprightly.

(Psalm 84:11)

"A good man leaves an inheritance to his children's children." God is a good God. "If you then, being evil, know how to give good gifts to your children, how much more will your Father who is in heaven give good things to those who ask Him!" (Matthew 7:11) God wants to bless us so that we will be a blessing to others.

I believe strongly that one of the reasons why God wants to transfer the wealth of sinners to the believers is that we can carry the gospel of the Kingdom to the ends of the earth. God is so much concerned about lost souls than anything else. When Jesus came, He came for all humanity. When He died, He died for all humankind.

> *For God so loved the world that He gave His only begotten Son, that whoever believes in Him should not perish but have everlasting life. For God did not send His Son into the world to condemn the world, but that the world through Him might be saved.*
>
> *(John 3:16-17)*

Jesus came to die for the entire world. But in His second coming, He is coming for His own – those who have accepted Him as their Lord and Saviour. God does not want any soul to perish. He loves all people. So, the Christians have a mandate to take the gospel to those who have not yet received it. We know for sure that it takes money to carry the gospel across nations and continents. King Solomon said, "…money answereth all things…" (Ecclesiastes 10:19 KJV). Without money the preaching of the gospel could be slow. Therefore, God who owns all the world would transfer the wealth the sinners to the saints to speed up the Good News.

As believers the desire to ask for the transfer wealth of the sinners must first be the purpose of preaching the gospel. God will not give us the wealth of sinners for our selfish interest or to enrich ourselves.

Walk in the Light of the Dream God has Given you

Any time you have a dream, any time you know your destiny, any time your calling is sure in your heart, those with no dream, no destiny and no confirmation of their calling will grow angry with you. But do not be discouraged, don't be afraid. We see through the Bible that Joseph was challenged to hang onto his dreams when his brothers conspired to kill him. The Book of Genesis described how they threw him in a pit and later sold him into slavery with the Ishmaelites, who in turn sold him to Potiphar in Egypt.

Then the brothers lied to their father and told him Joseph was dead. But you know something? The dream was still alive. Joseph was a key to the survival of Israel, and key people in strategic places who will obey the voice of God must be given the tools they need to accomplish His will. God has more in mind for you. We are the generation with a key purpose. God is calling a people to step into end time destiny – a financial destiny.

Your present circumstances have no bearing on your future with God. Don't look at what you can see with your natural eyes. If Joseph had, he would have given up long before he received the first great wealth transfer. We see through the Book of Genesis the troubles and pains Joseph went through. In all these atrocities God was with him. God was preparing Joseph to receive transfer of wealth from Pharaoh of Egypt. God will not transfer great amounts of wealth for ministry into the hands of those who doubt, lack character, or will not support the kingdom of God with their finances. God has a purpose for your wealth just as He had a purpose for Joseph's control of all the wealth of the greatest nation on the earth.

> *"Now therefore, let Pharaoh select a discerning and wise man, and set him over the land of Egypt. Let Pharaoh do this, and let him appoint officers over the land, to collect one-fifth of the produce of the land of Egypt in the seven plentiful years. And let them gather all the food of those good years that are coming, and store up grain under the authority of Pharaoh, and let them keep food in the cities. Then that food shall be as a reserve for the land for the seven years of famine which shall be in the land of Egypt, that the land may not perish during the famine."*

> *So the advice was good in the eyes of Pharaoh and in the eyes of all his servants. And Pharaoh said to his servants, "Can we find such a one as this, a man in whom is the Spirit of God?" Then Pharaoh said to Joseph, "Inasmuch as God has shown you all this, there is no one as discerning and wise as you. You shall be over my house, and all my people shall be ruled according to your word; only in regard to the throne will I be greater than you."*

> *And Pharaoh said to Joseph, "See, I have set you over all the land of Egypt." Then Pharaoh took his signet ring off his hand and put it on Joseph's hand; and he clothed him in garments of fine linen and put a gold chain around his*

neck. And he had him ride in the second chariot which he had; and they cried out before him, "Bow the knee!" So he set him over all the land of Egypt. Pharaoh also said to Joseph, "I am Pharaoh, and without your consent no man may lift his hand or foot in all the land of Egypt."

(Genesis 41:33-44)

Joseph rose from being a slave, and a prisoner, to being the ruler of all Egypt, second only to Pharaoh. He had authority over all the wealth of what was then the world's greatest kingdom and eventually gave him the ability to spare God's people from death during the terrible famine God brought upon the earth. God transferred the control of all Egypt's wealth into the hands of Joseph for a powerful purpose – to preserve God's children during the famine.

God will once again make a powerful great wealth transfer. The wealth of the wicked will be transferred into the hands of the righteous, but it will be done for a purpose. That purpose is to support the Great Commission. The scripture makes it clear what God intended to do in the end time: "And this gospel of the kingdom will be preached in all the world as a witness to all the nations, and then the end will come" (Matthew 24:14).

God Transferred the Wealth of Egypt to the Hebrews

God never intended the wealth of the world to belong in the hands of the ungodly. The wealth of the world belongs to God, and He desires to release it into the hands of His people. "For every beast of the forest is mine, and the cattle upon a thousand hills" (Psalm 50:10 KJV). From the very beginning of God's dealings with Abraham, when God entered a covenant with him, God poured His blessing upon him and prospered him. The transfer of the wealth of the wicked began when Abraham obeyed God and left his own country and entered Canaan.

God appeared to Abraham and told him that He was going to give him the land of Canaan. "And the LORD said to Abram, after Lot had separated from him: 'Lift your eyes now and look from the place where you are—northward, southward, eastward, and westward; for all the land which you see I give to you and your descendants forever'" (Genesis 13:14-15). Canaan, with all it wealth, did not belong to the Canaanites – the wealth of the wicked was being stored up for the just!

Later, when there was a great famine in Canaan, and Abraham went down into Egypt, there was a transfer of wealth. Pharaoh lavished gifts upon Abraham because of Sarah. When it is the time and season of God's blessing, it can come from any other sources. Pharaoh gave Abraham sheep, donkeys, camels, oxen, and servants. "He treated Abram well for her sake. He had sheep, oxen, male donkeys, male and female servants, female donkeys, and camels" (Genesis 12:16).

God blessed Abraham and Lot while they were in Egypt, their possessions were so great, that the land where they settled, in Bethel, was not big enough for them. They walked in God's abundance.

Then Abram went up from Egypt, he and his wife and all that he had, and Lot with him, to the South. Abram was very rich in livestock, in silver, and in gold. And he went on his journey from the South as far as Bethel, to the place where his tent had been at the beginning, between Bethel and Ai, to the place of the altar which he had made there at first. And there Abram called on the name of the LORD. Lot also, who went with Abram, had flocks and herds and tents. Now the land was not able to support them, that they might dwell together, for their possessions were so great that they could not dwell together.

(Genesis 13:2-6)

The Hebrews Plundered the Egyptian's Wealth

"Speak now in the hearing of the people, and let every man ask from his neighbor and every woman from her neighbor, articles of silver and articles of gold." And the LORD gave the people favor in the sight of the Egyptians. Moreover the man Moses was very great in the land of Egypt, in the sight of Pharaoh's servants and in the sight of the people.

(Exodus 11:2-3)

Through God's divine favour the wealth of the Egyptians was transferred to the Hebrews. Egypt became bankrupt. "The blessing of the LORD makes *one* rich, And He adds no sorrow with it" (Proverbs 10:22). God is about to unleash the most powerful supernatural transfer of wealth this world has ever known, and He is going to empower the Church with a supernatural financial endowment that will give the Church the ability to reach this entire world with the Gospel of Jesus Christ. All God wants from us is obedience. He never intended to depend on anything we possess, to use us.

This tremendous wealth of the Hebrews was eventually used to greatly glorify God in building the tabernacle and the Ark of the Covenant. "Then the LORD spoke to Moses, saying: 'Speak to the children of Israel, that they bring Me an offering. From everyone who gives it willingly with his heart you shall take My offering. And this *is* the offering which you shall take from them: gold, silver, and bronze; blue, purple, and scarlet *thread,* fine linen, and goats' *hair;* ram skins dyed red, badger skins, and acacia wood; oil for the light, and spices for the anointing oil and for the sweet incense; onyx stones, and stones to be set in the ephod and in the breastplate. And let them make Me a sanctuary, that I may dwell among them. According to all that I show you, *that is,* the pattern of the tabernacle and the pattern of all its furnishings, just so you shall make *it'''* (Exodus 25:1-9).

When God transfers the wealth of the wicked to you, are you prepared to use it for His glory?

❖

Bibliography

- Alex W. Ness. Copyright Agapre Publications Inc. Pefferlaw, Ontario L0E IN0, Canada

- Morris Cerullo. Giving and Receiving, Published for Morris Cerullo World Evangelism Copyright © 1995.

- Nelson, Thomas. The Holy Bible, New King James Version. Nashville, Tennessee USA: Broadman & Holman Publishers, Copyright © 1996

- Unless otherwise indicated, all scriptural quotations are taken from the New King James Version®. Copyright © 1982 by Thomas Nelson, Inc. Used by permission. All rights reserved.

- Scripture references marked CEV are taken from the Contemporary English Version® Copyright © 1995 American Bible Society. All rights reserved.

- Scripture references marked KJV are taken from the King James Version of the bible.

- Scripture marked NASB are taken from the New American Standard Bible®, Copyright © 1960, 1962, 1963, 1968, 1971, 1972, 1973, 1975, 1977, 1995 by The Lockman Foundation. Used by permission.

- Scripture quotations marked NIV are taken from THE HOLY BIBLE, NEW INTERNATIONAL VERSION®, NIV®

❖

Ministry Profile

Apostle Dr. Benjamin Ayim Asare is an anointed minister of God with a strong deliverance flow, which is evident in all facets of his ministry. He is the president of **World Missions Ministries (WMM)** and the Senior Pastor of the **Followers of Christ International Church (FOCIC)** Novara, Italy.

Apostle Benjamin is the coordinator and president of the Followers of Christ International Church. A member of **"Chiese Elim in Italia"** and holds Italian Ministerial Licenses "Ministro di culto." He is also on the board of LifeStyle International Christian University (LICU) as an Executive Director, faculty member and is responsible for National Growth. On May 7th, 2013, Dr. Alan Pateman appointed Dr. Ayim Asare as an Executive Board Member of the International Apostolic Accreditation Council (IAAC) where he is responsible for the Association of Professionals.

Dr. Benjamin is a conference speaker, church planter, leadership mentor. He is an itinerant minister who ministers to organizations as well as groups and churches and ministers throughout nations.

In May 2010 Apostle Ayim Asare established the **"School of Ministry for Potential Leaders" (SOMFPL)** the aim is to provide training/seminar programs for ordinary people to potential leaders for the work of ministry, and that is to help them to identify their calling and ministry. This is the purpose and burden of the pastor and his leaders.

In 2015 Apostle Dr. Benjamin Ayim Asare established the **"All Believers International Convention" (ABIC),** the purpose of this yearly event is to develop a Network of Ministers for a cutting-edge relationship that will bring unity, encouragements, support and sharpens our gifts and callings in a tremendous way, simply because no one has ever been successful in life alone.

Dr. Benjamin is the owner of **"BENCOM Publication,"** publishing and distribution materials such as "Salvation is Free" for churches as Sunday school tools in English and in Italian and has authored several books.

This anointed man of God encourages thousands to answer the call of God through the teaching of the Word and dynamic demonstration of the Holy Spirit. His unique ability to identify the God-given gifting, calling and anointing upon God's people, through his proven dynamic teachings, draws the hearts of the people to our Lord and Saviour Jesus Christ as God's purpose is activated in their lives. Clearly, minds are renewed, lives are transformed and hearts are drawn to our heavenly Father as God's power and authority is magnificently displayed.

Academic Background: Benjamin attended several colleges throughout his training. He attended Placid Secretarial Academy (Ghana), World Impact Bible Institute (Canada), Florida Christian University (USA) where he earned a Bachelor of Ministry B.Min. and LifeStyle International Christian University (Italy), where he also earned a Master of Arts in Theology M.A. and Doctor of

Ministry in Theology D.Min, (2013). Furthermore, he has been awarded an Honorary Degree of Doctor of Divinity D.D. from LifeStyle International Christian University.

Apostle Dr. Benjamin Ayim Asare lives in Novara, Italy with his family.

www.benjaminayimasareministries.com
bayimasare@yahoo.it
focicatmissions@yahoo.com

❖

To Contact the Author

Please email:

Followers of Christ International Church
c/o Apostle Benjamin Ayim Asare
Via Ghiberti, 1
Novara 28100
ITALY

Email: bayimasare@yahoo.it or
focicatmissions@yahoo.com

*Please include your prayer requests
and comments when you write.*

❖

Other Books

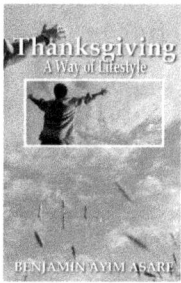

Thanksgiving, A Way of Lifestyle

Within this book, Apostle Benjamin Ayim Asare will help you to discover the importance of thanksgiving and every bumped crop you have attained in life. You will also discover how to appreciate people whom God uses to bless your life. Everything we enjoy in the present and coming age is a gift from God worthy of thanksgiving. All people including non Christians and Christians enjoy the blessings of the Lord.

ISBN: 978-0-9575775-2-7, Pages: 92,
Format: Paperback, Published: 2017

Discover your Ministry in the Local Church

When you begin to develop the ability to sever all alternatives and give total concentration and focus to the things that interests you most, you will discover incredible and remarkable success. Dr. Benjamin Ayim has provided a tool which will open your understanding to discover the purpose, the need and the practical approach of the ministry of helps in the local church.

ISBN: 978-0-9575775-1-0, Pages: 153,
Format: Paperback, Published: 2016

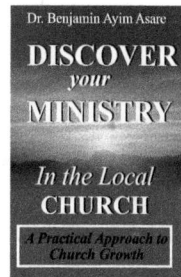

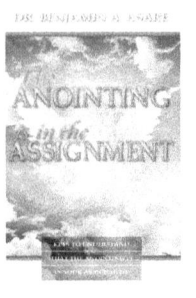

The Anointing is in the Assignment

The purpose of the anointing is for you as a Christian to live a victorious life and to witness the gospel message of Jesus Christ effectively. God wants to take ordinary people and work supernaturally through them to bring about a mighty move of His power, just the way He worked through His Son, Jesus Christ.

ISBN: 978-1-909132-07-8, Pages: 220, Format: Paperback, Published: 2015

The Hand of the Diligent Will Rule

God has given us His resources of Time and Talent to receive money. You must remember that work is important to God. God values the work you do, because your work or job is equal to your time, talent and gifting. These gifts are God's resources and therefore God will not be happy with any of His children who take work for granted. Your work requires diligence, and excellent attitude determines good quality productivity.

ISBN: 978-0-957577-50-3, Pages: 120, Format: Paperback, Published: 2013

Life is a Priceless Treasure

As you look beyond your time on earth, which in comparison with eternity, is just a brief moment, you will be assured that heaven, is your home. Time spent on earth is short. Yet this short time is very essential because it prepares you to receive everything needed in heaven.

BENCOM Publications, Pages: 47, Format: Paperback, Published: 2008

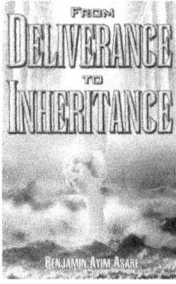

From Deliverance to Inheritance

In this revolutionary book on deliverance, you will discover, understand and know the enemy, and know how you can take your strength in the Lord to overcome him in order to possess your inheritance.

BENCOM Publications, Pages: 129, Format: Paperback, Published: 2008

The Unfolding Mysteries of the Voice of the Blood

The Unfolding Mysteries of the Voice of the Blood contains volumes of powerful and clear revelations about the biblical blood covenant. There is power in the Blood. The author gives some amazing truth about the voice of the Blood of Christ, which will build your faith as you go through the pages of this book.

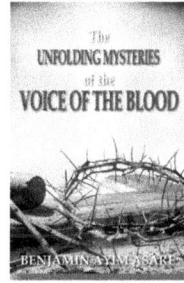

ISBN: 978-0-9575775-4-1, Pages: 108, Format: Paperback, Published: 2018

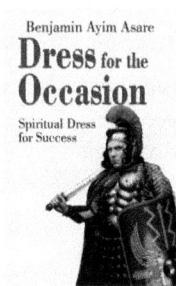

Dress for the Occasion

The objective of this book is that the Christian will understand the principles and how to take our stand in the Word of God against the devil. As you go through the pages of the book, you will be moved from revelation to manifestation; equip and wage your strategic warfare victoriously.

ISBN: 978-0-9574775-7-2, Pages: 84, Format: Paperback, Published: 2022

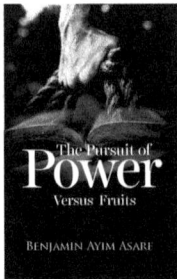

The Pursuit of Power Versus Fruits

This book will give the life principles of ordinary people who finished well. Each person provides a clue about what God values for our lives. Therefore we need to pursue fruit than power. Obedience is the right choice we must follow. Pursuing power rather than fruit would lead to self gratification then eventually to self-destruction.

ISBN: 978-09575775-6-5, Pages: 71, Format: Paperback, Published: 2019

- Italian Books -

La Vita è un Tesoro Inestimabile

Quando guardi al di là del tuo tempo sulla terra, che in confronto all' eternità è solo un breve momento, sarai sicuro che il cielo sarà la tua casa. Il tempo vissuto sulla terra è breve. Tuttavia, questi breve periodo di tempo è una cosa molto indispensabile, perchè ti prepara a ricevere tutte le cose di cui hai bisogno nel cielo.

ISBN 978-88-87511-90-1, Pages: 44, Format: Paperback, Published: 2009

Dalla Liberazione all'Eredità

Libertà significa semplicemente uscire da una prigione o da problemi di legami economici, sociali e politici. Gesù fu mandato intenzionalmente da Dio per liberarci dal dominio del nemico.

ISBN 978-88-87511-85-7, Pages: 96, Format: Paperback, Published: 2009

❖

All Books Available

at

BENCOM PUBLICATIONS

Email: bayimasare@yahoo.it or
focicatmissions@yahoo.com

*Also Available from Amazon.com
and other retail outlets.*

www.ingramcontent.com/pod-product-compliance
Lightning Source LLC
Chambersburg PA
CBHW071614040426
42452CB00008B/1340